AT THE HEART OF EVERY STORM LIES

THE POWER OF GOD TO **CHANGE YOUR WORLD**

STORM™

CHASER

THE TERRY LAW STORY

JAMES GILBERT

Storm Chaser: The Terry Law Story
Copyright © 2014 by Terry Law

Published by Terry Law: Storm Chaser LLC
www.stormchaser.org

Library of Congress Cataloging-in-Publication Data
Applied for

ISBN: 978-1-50571-399-2

Printed in the United States of America

Design: Peter Gloege | LOOK Design Studio

Editorial development and creative design support by Ascent:
www.itsyourlifebethere.com

Follow Terry:
TerryLawSC @TerryLawSC StormChaser.org

To John and Elizabeth Sherrill,
who set the storytelling standard,
and
to Millennials everywhere,
who want to make a difference.
Here is your template.

PROLOGUE

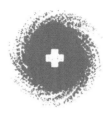

INSIDE A BEECHCRAFT CHARTER PLANE streaking across the sky toward Baghdad, Iraq, Terry Law was steeling himself for the danger that lay ahead, and feeling shaken by what he had left behind. He had been fine until two days ago in western Canada, when his family bade him farewell.

Terry had flown to St. Eugene's Mission Resort in the Canadian Rockies to perform the outdoor wedding of his niece, Lorian. So important was it to the Taylors that Uncle Terry officiate, that they had held the ceremony earlier than scheduled just to have him there. Even at that, Terry and his youngest daughter, Laurie, had been forced to leave early in order to catch their flights at Calgary International Airport.

Lorian and her family had shed more than a few tears when Terry said goodbye, not so much because he was leaving—they were used to that—but because of where he was going. "Be careful over there in…Baghdad," Lyle Taylor had cautioned. The family's resident jester had choked with emotion as he said it, and for the past 48 hours the break in Lyle's voice had followed Terry half way around the world.

As he scoured the sea of sand four miles beneath him, Terry was acutely aware that planes like this one were clay pigeons for snipers. *This really is dangerous,* he told himself, as if for the first time. Of course he already knew it was a hazardous mission, so the thought wasn't new. But the feeling was. For a good twenty years it had been easier to bury his emotions, to lose them in the whirlwind of preaching engagements, plane flights, and frequent missions into various danger zones around the globe. But as perilous as his previous ministry had been, he realized now that he was just minutes from beginning the most dangerous assignment of his life, and Lyle's words reminded him that this time it was entirely possible that he might never see his family again.

Where are they? he wondered about the snipers he had heard so much about. With only one commercial flight per day flying into Baghdad International, a private flight like his could draw attention. Then again, maybe they were lying in wait along the highway into town. *Surely the General has planned for that,* he reassured himself, and fast-forwarded his thoughts to the single purpose of his journey.

How in the world does an American preacher get a Muslim nation to rewrite its constitution? he asked himself for the umpteenth time. In two days he would come face to face with Iraq's prime minister, to intercede for the people's right to religious freedom, which, along with the lives of thousands of Christians, hung precariously in the balance. Centuries of hatred and prejudice against "Christ-followers" lay blanketed as thick and widespread as the sands below, and the slightest ill wind could stir up a storm of persecution and wholesale slaughter. Someone had to stop it from happening, to speak up now, while there was still time.

But why me? he thought. *Why not some diplomat, or at least some neutral party? Why does it come down to somebody so unquali-fied, a guy with all the wrong credentials?* Terry felt his blood drain a little; he was being scolded by his own common sense. *Too late to worry about that now, Law. You're the one who chased this storm and now you're caught in the teeth of it, just like you were in Afghanistan. And China before that, and Russia, and....*

Suddenly the old saying was true: Terry's life really was flashing before him. Mental images of himself as a boy, splashing around in the driving rain, chasing the thunder and lightning—he had always loved the stuff that made other kids run for cover. And setting off dynamite to find water back on Ed's ranch when he was in his early twenties; that beat Bible school any day. Then again, almost any-thing beat Bible school when it came to excitement. Sure, he could have taken one of the churches up on their offer and probably be safe and comfortable in a parsonage somewhere in western Canada right now. Safe, comfortable, but also completely bored and won-dering: Is this all there is to my life? Is this what I was made for?

Terry smiled, then refocused, as the azure waters of Lake Habbaniya came into view, and beyond them the city of Fallujah. Ten minutes later the veteran preacher and his assistant of 30 years, Joel Vesanen, would pass over Abu Ghraib and then quickly dive—literally, he had been warned—into the firestorm that was greater Baghdad, Iraq. If there were such a thing as hell on earth in this August of 2005, Iraq's largest city would be its furnace. In the four months since the Battle of Abu Ghraib, suicide bombers had attacked the capital with increasing frequency. Osama bin Laden and his Al Qaeda cohorts clearly did not want the country's parlia-ment to ratify the new constitution that had been drafted back in January. Yet it was that very document that had brought Terry here, into the mother of all storms.

He looked over at Joel, who had stood beside him so often when a more sensible man would have run. Only three years earlier the two had been nearly stoned to death by an Afghan mob, and in times past they had been known to smuggle dissidents out of some countries and Bibles into others. Once they had even sneaked bags of rice across a frozen river from China into North Korea, a crime that would have landed them in one of dictator Kim Jong Il's labor camps.

"You might want to tighten your seatbelts, gentlemen," said the captain. The South African had been the only pilot in Amman, Jordan, willing to fly Terry and Joel to Baghdad. "We're going into a 2G spin."

They were almost four miles directly above the runway at Baghdad International Airport when the plane entered its intentional spiral. The pilot was performing something called a corkscrew landing, a tactic he employed for the same reasons a football player returning a kickoff weaves right and left to dodge opposition tackles. In this case, however, the shoulders of the opposing players bore missile launchers instead of padding.

Less than ten minutes later, the Beechcraft had plummeted from 20,000 feet above sea level to exactly 114, the altitude of Baghdad International's runway. As soon as her props and wheels ceased turning, the plane's doors flung open and Terry and Joel strode rapidly towards the terminal. The morning temperature had already reached 110 degrees, but out on the tarmac it was nearing 130, and they were as eager to escape the heat as to avoid snipers.

Once they were inside the massive, nearly abandoned terminal, bodyguards bearing AK-47 assault rifles whisked the duo across white marble floors, past unmanned immigration booths, and out the door into a plain gray Toyota Corolla that sat between twin black Land Cruisers assigned to run interference on their ten-mile journey into Baghdad.

"Hello, my friends," said the driver, as Terry climbed into the front seat of the purposely nondescript car and Joel took the backseat. General Georges Sada, former assistant commander of Saddam Hussein's air force against his own will, and now senior advisor to Iraq's Prime Minister, extended a hand to each man before signaling "go" to the bodyguard behind the wheel of the lead SUV. All of the guards, like Sada himself, were Assyrian Christians who had pledged their lives to protect him. It was a commitment they might be called upon to keep at any moment, since they were exiting the world's most dangerous airport for a high-speed drive along its most perilous road.

As the small convoy entered the deserted airport expressway, Sada reached into the Toyota's glove box and pulled out a loaded Smith & Wesson .38 revolver. "Take this," said the general, passing the gun to Terry. "If I need it, hand it to me." Terry cradled the weapon nervously. He was a preacher, not a fighter, but "riding shotgun" was quickly taking on new meaning.

They had driven less than a mile, and the lead SUV had already zoomed out of sight, no mean feat, since the little Toyota itself was nearing triple-digit speed. The general had adopted the same zigzag pattern—left-right-left-right—as the Beechcraft's pilot. "We are making it harder for rocket-propelled grenades to hit us," he explained, and suddenly Terry found driving wildly at high speeds a perfectly sensible idea.

The highway ended and a stoplight loomed ahead, but the Toyota pressed on. Terry searched the floor with his feet, as if feeling around for a hidden passenger brake. Sada smiled and calmly barreled on, knowing that his advance guard had sufficiently brought traffic to a standstill. "Snipers wait at the intersections," he said in his clipped accent, as they zoomed past the red light at 80 miles per hour. "They look for uniforms or white skin."

Reaching Baghdad proper, the convoy avoided the city's center and sped towards a safer, less hectic suburb on her outskirts. Within minutes they had arrived at the general's residence, and his bodyguards joined the contingent already stationed around its perimeter. Soon Sada had seated his guests at a dining table, where Terry savored his cup of black tea and calm surroundings more than he might ever have expected.

The day's journey from Amman had been even more harrowing than the previous year's trip up north, when he had wound up fleeing for his life across the border into Turkey. That was the week he had made the promise he was keeping now. "Please help us," implored the little nun at a Catholic orphanage. "Our new constitution is being drafted with no provision for religious freedom. Without it we Christians will suffer. You must help us."

"I'm just a preacher from Oklahoma," he had objected, not from modesty but because it was true. "What can I do?"

But the mother superior was persistent, and eventually he had vowed to help. Now here he was, after a stop at the White House a few days earlier, ready to take his case directly to Prime Minister Ibrahim Al-Jaafari, who, thanks to the General, had consented to hear him in two more days. Armed with some good advice from Washington, Terry had composed a specific proposal to include a religious-freedom article in Iraq's new constitution. He also carried with him nearly 20,000 signed petitions demonstrating American, Canadian and British support. Still, he felt in over his head.

The unlikely ambassador finished his tea and stood to his feet to look around the room at the concussion cracks that marred the walls of Sada's home, costly souvenirs of the "shock and awe" that ended Saddam Hussein's 24-year chokehold on the country. The stomach-churning landing and dizzying drive behind him, he wished he could skip a day and get to the job at hand. But his wild ride was not over. In truth, he had landed in the middle of a colossal spiritual storm, a dark and roiling cloud more ominous than any he had faced before.

"Congratulations," General Sada would tell him a day from now. "You and I have just become Al Qaeda's two most wanted men in Iraq."

Later, those words would come to haunt him. Here he was, walking into the maelstrom. Again. Knowing it was imperative that he be here. Knowing he was not equipped in any professional or political way to be the man to face down titanic forces set on destruction—and also knowing God had chosen him for the assignment. He never ceased to be amazed at God's calling and the empowering grace he knew he would be given to face the task at hand...and hopefully come out alive.

Why are you so surprised? he thought, half-smiling. This had been the pattern of his life—to chase a storm until he found its vortex and then walk straight into it because *that* was invariably where he found God's power. It was why he instinctively chased thunder as a child and committed petty crimes as a teen, until eventually he ran into his Maker, who, rather than stop him, taught him to chase the right kind of storm, to find its eye, and to stay there. And although the ensuing decades had seen him become a man of considerable achievement, tragic miscalculation, and deep sorrow, Terry Law had become convinced of this truth: Jesus reigns from the center of every storm, and "rules in the midst of his enemies."

And now he was in Baghdad to prove it once again.

CHAPTER 1

CLOUDED HEART

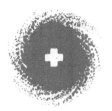

HOW ON EARTH was he going to hide his true identity?

Terry squinted at the lingering Prince Albert sun, wishing he still lived in Parkside. It wasn't just because the little town was still home in his heart, nor because he and Murray would probably have been racing across the Saskatchewan prairie on some new adventure. No, he wished he was *there* in Parkside, because it would mean not being stuck *here* in Prince Albert, on Central Avenue in broad daylight, *here* at a Pentecostal street meeting where—at any moment—somebody like Brian Albright, one of his enemies, might see him and recognize him.

"Have you committed your life to Christ?" Bert Law, Terry's father, was preaching to the small group of people who had stopped to see what was going on.

One man scratched his chin and yawned. A lady next to him was getting teary. Any minute now and she might break out crying.

Terry shifted uncomfortably and searched the street to see if Brian, or any of the other guys from school who loved to torment him, was in sight. He could hear their taunts already. *"Hey, shorty, are you and your old man 'getting people saved'?"*

He'll tell everyone at school, and I'll never be able to live it down, Terry thought. And if it weren't the bully Brian it would be someone else. A couple of kids he knew would hear the singing or his father's preaching and stop for a minute to snicker. And sure as anything that would be the exact moment his dad would call him and his sister, Lois, to come to the front and sing "We'll Understand it Better By and By," while their mom played the accordion.

Then everyone would know the embarrassing secret he was hiding: Terry Law was the *Pentecostal* preacher's son. And they'd trot off, looking back over their shoulders mocking him. By Monday morning, every eighth grader at King George would have heard it: Law is a holy roller! He's one of those weirdos from that little church on 10th Street where people shake and scream and swing from the chandeliers. He imagined himself walking down the halls at school, listening to their jeers. "Hey, Terry, do you have the Holy Ghost? C'mon, speak in tongues for us, ay!"

The bored-looking man was still staring at Terry's dad, and the teary woman was still dabbing at her eyes.

"Give your life to Christ now, friend," Bert Law insisted, his voice growing impassioned. "You don't know if you have tomorrow."

Why does it have to be right in front of City Hall? Terry flinched, gritting his teeth. Carefully, trying not to be noticed, he snuck to the back row of the small choir his dad had recruited for the occasion.

Being a Christian is so embarrassing, Terry thought. Then he felt guilty for thinking it. He hated this feeling—this feeling of conflict he always carried inside about his faith. *Okay, so I'm a Christian. Do I have to announce it to the world? Why does that have to be my job?* There were so many other things he'd rather be doing.

At least it was 7 p.m. and the streets weren't as crowded as they had been that afternoon. Most of his buddies were likely at home having supper. But, taking no chances, Terry nudged his way in among the taller men, as far back from the street as possible. Brother Poole, an ancient, gray-haired member of the choir smiled down at him—which made Terry feel even more guilty.

He probably thinks I like being here, helping to spread the gospel. He has no clue I'd rather be dead right now.

"*This*...is your hour of decision!" Bert Law said, in a voice as loud and impassioned as polite Canadian preachers got. "*This...is your time!*"

Terry looked over at his father, who looked natty and confident in his black suit and tie—then glanced up and down the street again. In another minute the choir would sing while his father led the teary lady in "the sinner's prayer."

Dad's not the least bit embarrassed, he thought, staring at his father. Bert's black hair and matching horn-rimmed glasses sometimes cast him as severe, but his pulpit grin and genuine enthusiasm for preaching the gospel always won over his listeners, which is what this Saturday evening was all about, and why it was happening downtown. *Win the lost at any cost!*—that was the motto of any self-respecting preacher in the Pentecostal Assemblies of Canada, and his dad seemed better at it than most. It was what had gotten him the invitation to take the reins here at Prince Albert's Evangelistic Centre.

It wasn't just the street preaching that bothered Terry, though. It was... *everything* about his dad. He was better than most men at almost everything—like being a crack shot with a rifle. Who else could kill a wolf, running at full tilt, from 300 yards? That memory was still very fresh, like every vivid incident involving Bert Law....

* * *

They had been on their way to Leask that day when Bert spotted the four-legged poacher. He knew it must be the one that had been killing livestock on local farms, and had pulled the car to a fast stop. He grabbed his rifle from the back seat and rushed Terry out of the driver's door, so that the car concealed them. "Watch this," his dad had said. Then he propped his right arm on the hood and stuck a wet finger in the air to measure the wind. The wolf was just a moving speck in the distance, and Terry could barely see it.

The sudden explosion right next to Terry had made him jump. And out past the tree line, the wolf dropped like a rock.

His dad had killed it with a single shot.

Right then and there, Bert Law had become Superman. As far as Terry was concerned there was nothing his father couldn't do—well. At Bible school, he'd helped build the dorm that housed him, transformed a decrepit town hall into his first church, was a decent rancher, and even sutured his own big toe—without anesthetic—after splitting it open with an axe one winter while chopping firewood....

* * *

At Bert's signal, the choir began. Beside Terry, old Brother Poole was rumbling out the bass line....

Softly and tenderly Jesus is calling,
Calling for you and for me...

The woman had stepped forward as soon as the song began, and Bert was praying with her in front of the whole group—just as Terry had feared.

Or not *feared* so much as…loathed. *Why does he have to be good at everything?* One of the best things you could be in their Pentecostal world was a great preacher and "soul winner."

There's no way I can ever do what dad does. He has no fear of what people think.

And that, when Terry was honest with himself, was the real problem. If he was to speak about Jesus among his buddies at school he'd be running face first into a hail of insults, laughter and abuse. And *that* was just not going to happen.

The woman had finished praying the sinner's prayer with Bert now, and was wiping her eyes, while her new pastor waited through the song's chorus, to see if anyone else would respond.

Come home, come home,
You who are weary come ho-o-ome.

If it was possible to become invisible, Terry would have disappeared. In comparison to his dad's boldness and many talents, he felt nearly invisible and totally insignificant already. His father was so intimidating it cancelled out any inspiration Terry might otherwise have felt.

I know dad expects me to witness to all my friends, Terry thought. *But I can't. I just can't.*

Earnestly, tenderly, Jesus is calling,
Calling, O sinner, come home!

Terry mouthed the words, knowing in his heart that for him they were just words. He could never be a "soul winner"—never measure up to his dad no matter how hard he tried. When he had gotten all A's and a lone B on his report card, "You can do better," had been Bert's only response. When a schoolyard bully had boxed his ears, his bruises had elicited not sympathy, but a cold—"Go learn how to box."

* * *

That night, as Terry crawled into bed, more images haunted him. His face felt hot against the pillow at the memory of a hunting trip he and his dad had taken, heading out across the prairie, looking for antelope. What could be better than hunting with your dad? But everything can go wrong fast when you're riding with your rifle's safety off.

Bert had spotted a buck and stomped on the brakes. "Get out and take a shot. Quick, before he runs."

Terry's whole body had begun to quiver, and in his haste to open the door and hop out, he'd pulled the trigger.

The blast shattered a nearby rock, spraying bits of stone shrapnel everywhere. A piece struck Terry in the knee, causing him to grab it and start hollering.

Bert raced around the car, thinking Terry was shot and seriously injured—then silently shook his head when he saw the truth.

The hunt was over then. Clearly, Bert Law thought his son was never going to amount to much. Terry was sure he could hear his thoughts. *Can't hunt. Too timid to testify…* And ever since then Terry had remembered the sting, not from the rock but from his father's eyes.

What he did not see then, as he settled into sleep, was the fact that that look of disgust and dismissal was the same one he now saw in the mirror every day. What he couldn't quite hear was the silent message that played over and over in the back of his mind: *How could someone weak like you ever do great things in life—let alone for God?*

* * *

The next day, and every day after, Terry was left with a question playing at the edges of his thoughts: *Dad has found his place as a respected preacher in his denomination. How am I ever going to find where I fit in this world? I want to do great things with my life, too—but what?*

But the future was a long way off. Right now, Terry's life had taken a really bad turn with the move to Prince Albert. The kids at King George School laughed at religion, even the ones who went to church on Sunday. And since the student body outnumbered the entire population of his former home town, laughing with them seemed like the only way for a scrawny country preacher's kid to assimilate. Church was now a complete embarrassment. So following that whole avenue—becoming a preacher like his dad—was not an option. Not even close.

And besides that, Terry reasoned, Christianity itself was just boring. Right now it was making his life miserable, since according to his denomination nearly everything Terry thought of as fun was labeled a sin and could make you miss the rapture if Jesus came while you were doing it.

For instance, there was no transgression in the world worse than going to the movies. And the problem was, Terry had been hooked on them ever since taking some change from his paper route one day to buy a ticket. It was too risky to go often, but once in a while he couldn't resist, and would sneak into the Orpheum down on Central Avenue to see a James Dean or John Wayne picture.

Something about the big screen captivated him. It looked like some giant window on the world, and he wished he could just walk up and step right through it and see it all for himself. His own world was so small by comparison, and he sat there in the dark theater, completely enthralled by every adventure, right up until the credits rolled at the end.

But every time, as soon as the house lights would come up, fear grabbed at his chest. He was about to walk out the door into the bright sunlight—and someone from his dad's congregation might see him leaving that evil place! Worse than that, what if Jesus really had come while he was inside and he'd been left behind?

There were other fears, too. One was the fear that his folks or someone from church would catch him sneaking a cigarette with one of the boys from school. It was as though his life was a tug-of-war and his soul was the rope.

Worst of all, he thought, God could see what a fake he was, because in his heart the "wrong" side was winning.

It didn't help that Terry's frequent visits back to Parkside, to hang out with his best friend, Murray, made for a lopsided contest. And Parkside was where Terry loved to escape. There he could be his *other* self… the kid his parents knew nothing about.

* * *

The little prairie town of Parkside, less than an hour west of Prince Albert, was Terry's personal paradise. "This is my town," he had told his mother one day when he was just seven. "I never want to live anywhere else." With a population hovering around 130, Parkside was small enough that everyone knew everyone else. In short, it was any little boy's safe, perfect playground.

Even street meetings had been fun back then, especially down in Leask, where Bert wanted to start a branch church. For one thing, anybody making music on a Saturday night was welcome out on the prairie, where entertainment choices were limited. Plus, pastors were more respected in small towns, so being a preacher's kid had a touch of celebrity attached to it, especially if you could sing. All the group had to do in Leask was to take its place on the concrete sidewalk and start singing. Then people would come out and stand in the dirt tire tracks and listen. Terry and his little sister, Lois, could harmonize well even at ages seven and five, so their father nearly always featured them, along with Ann's playing on the accordion. After the last song, Bert would preach and offer to pray with anyone who wanted to come forward after a final benediction. And when it was over, everyone would say how good Terry and Lois sounded together. Best of all, youth groups from churches in other towns would join them, and nobody laughed at anybody else for being religious.

But all this was before the embarrassment of being a Pentecostal and the pressure to measure up to his dad had made being a Christian distasteful.

The real draw in Parkside, besides being out of everyone's critical eye, was Terry's best friend, Murray Dahl.

Murray's dad had given him an old Model-T that the two drove up and down the back roads whenever Terry came to visit. Neither set of parents had a problem with it, because every boy in farm country was driving an old truck or a tractor on his dad's farm by age twelve. But what they didn't know was that their sons' joyrides frequently included after-dark beer and cigarettes at the local cemetery, where older teenagers regularly gathered to smoke and drink and practice the art of "cussing." Those three acts in particular constituted rites of passage in the Age of Elvis, and before he had even turned 13, Terry knew them well, right down to the Sen-Sens he used to cleanse his beery breath and the green, Christmas-tree shaped air fresheners he rubbed against his clothing to mask the smell of burnt tobacco.

His parents might have been fooled, but in Terry's conscience an intolerant, Marlboro-hating God was always catching, trying, and condemning him. From well-meaning Sunday School teachers to fiery youth-camp evangelists, the message was clear: salvation is as easily lost as found, especially by means of smoking, drinking, or frequenting such worldly venues as pool halls, dance halls, and movie theaters. It was as if someone had discovered a list called "Terry Law's Favorite Things to Do," and made it the official road map to hell. Even his mother provided no comfort.

The daughter of an impoverished wheat farmer, Ann Law was cut from the same tough cloth as husband Bert. She had even delivered a few sermons back in her school days at Bethel Bible Institute in Saskatoon. And while she may have lacked her husband's finesse in the pulpit, Ann's devotion to God and to her denomination's code of conduct proved a formidable force at home. Not that she didn't love her three children—Terry knew she did. But sometimes he wondered if the only Bible verse she knew was the one from the *Book of Numbers* that says, "Be sure your sins will find you out." *Or maybe it's because I have so many sins*, he often thought. *Maybe I'll just never be good enough for her or Dad. I know I'm not good enough for God.*

And what about that "sinners saved by grace" scripture his dad was always quoting? What *was* grace anyway?

Maybe it's some kind of probation, like, "OK, Terry, I'll let you into my heaven, but one slip-up and you're out."

Whatever grace was, it sure seemed to have a lot of conditions attached.

The sense of condemnation and inferiority that had grown within Terry so quickly after moving to Prince Albert erupted in earnest with the onset of puberty, and his increased interest in sex compounded the whole mess. Emotions, hormones, and the struggle to feel like he measured up to other guys—these all hit at once, triggering an even bigger chaos in Terry's soul. After all, *good* Christian boys didn't think about sex—did they?

Occasionally an adult would ask Terry the question all children are asked, especially ministers' sons: "What do you want to be when you grow up?" Answering "a preacher like my dad" had been easy when he was little, but now the pimply preteen found himself drawing a complete blank. He only knew what he *didn't* want to be: He didn't want to feel condemned, he didn't want to feel inferior, and he especially didn't want to be poor, because that was the most humiliating thing of all about being a Pentecostal pastor's son.

He had learned that lesson the hard way one Halloween back in Parkside, when he and Murray went trick-or-treating. It was fun wearing a mask and collecting lots of candy—fun, that is, until one of the neighborhood families had recognized him from his clothing. It was a shirt and pants they had tossed into the missionary basket at church.

Remembering the moment devastated him now as much as it had that night, but it had also ignited a fire that hardened his resolve like a brick cured in a kiln: the grown-up Terry Law would never be poor again. For that matter, if being a Christian meant being poor, then maybe he wouldn't be a Christian either. Somehow he'd get rich, and finally be free from all the stupid rules that kept his life boring and his family poor. Somehow…

What do I want to be? he began asking himself, and for the next several months the question dominated his thoughts. Would he be a farmer like his dad? No, he could never be as good as his father, not at ranching or hunting or construction, or anything else. And he *especially* did not want to be a Pentecostal preacher. No, there had to be something else, something prestigious and powerful, some other calling people would respect. Eventually— perhaps inevitably—the word "politician" came to mind, since as a newspaper boy he was dispensing headlines dominated by them, and was already aware of a local lawyer, John Diefenbaker, who was well on his way to becoming Canada's 13th Prime Minister.

"What would be the best way to get into politics?" Terry asked one of his teachers at King George School.

"Most politicians start out by becoming attorneys," came the reply.

That was all it took. Terry latched onto the idea and began telling himself, *I'm going to be a lawyer.* He knew he was good academically and could think on his feet. That was it! He could picture himself like Perry Mason, Erle Stanley Gardner's famous counsel for the defense, pacing the courtroom floor, convincing juries, and saving innocent people's lives. And of course, in the process he would get rich, move through the tiers of elective office, and maybe even become the Prime Minister of Canada.

He dreamed about wearing expensive suits, and could see himself driving a big Ford Meteor, the one with the chrome bullet grille. The main objective, of course, was just to get out of Prince Albert and move around in important circles, and look good doing it. And one thing was certain: Attorney Terry Law would never again wear anything that came out of a missionary basket.

By the time the school year ended and his fourteenth birthday had come and gone, he felt like life was good and about to get even better. Summer was coming, and with it Terry's favorite part of the year: camp meeting at Nanoose Bay in British Columbia!

If there was any place he could escape and hide from his life it was summer camp. Or so he thought.

But by refusing to search for God's purpose and letting his own ego call the shots, Terry had opened himself to a deeper level of inner turbulence than he could ever have imagined, one that could never be calmed by money, big cars and expensive, tailored suits. In fact, the opposite was true. Such shallow appetites only stir the inner storm, so that sooner or later it is bound to create havoc.

CHAPTER 2

REBEL WITH A CALL

FOR ALL HIS REBELLIOUS WAYS, Terry had always loved going to church camp. And since his dad had recently moved the family from clay-baked Saskatchewan further west to take a pastorate in beautiful British Columbia, he was sure the camp this summer at Nanoose Bay would be the best ever.

Sure, there were revival meetings and preachers every morning and evening in the main "tabernacle" hall, but the camp also had a ball field and its very own beach on the Pacific coast, which meant he would have a solid week of good, sweaty fun that even Pentecostals didn't consider sinful. Besides, he could always sneak a couple of cigarettes out in the woods.

As his dad's new Ford pulled into camp, Terry looked out the window, and at once two feelings began wrestling inside of him.

One was the sense that he'd gone to heaven. Compared to the Living Waters camp back in Saskatchewan, this place was a paradise of blue waters, salt breezes, emerald green grass, and assorted mismatched cabins and picnic tables strewn beneath a canopy of towering fir trees.

Could he find what he really wanted here?

Terry helped his dad shift luggage from the car to the family's cabin, and then slipped away on his own, past the trees and across the ball field until he reached the water's edge. There was a boat docked about 800 yards across the bay.

Wonder if I could swim from here to there, he asked himself.

The other sense rose in him—the restless feeling he could never get away from. At the surface level it showed itself in the crazy things he did. Right now, he was thinking that daring to swim across the rough waters of the bay would be a great way to make his mark on this place, doing something the bigger guys would never attempt. Back at Living Waters Terry had set the whole camp talking about him by swimming all the way across Lake Manitou and back.

Terry grinned as he remembered his father yelling at him when he crawled back on shore. "You could have drowned!" Bert had shouted, while everybody else stood around *tsk-tsking* and shaking their heads at his foolhardiness.

What's the big deal? Terry wondered, feeling proud of his feat. Lake Manitou was so salty that he couldn't have drowned in its super-buoyant waters if he tried.

He looked over at the boat dock and recalculated his prospects. He could probably do the distance, but the choppy waters might get him into real trouble. *Not enough salt anyway,* he finally decided, with a shake of his head. *But there's got to be something.*

Terry had been there ten minutes and was already restless. In fact, lately he found himself restless all the time. That was the deeper problem. He loved a challenge. He *needed* a challenge. But everything in his world was about control and containment. There was pretty much nothing that he found exciting that wasn't also forbidden.

How would he find what he really needed—a challenge big enough—here at camp meeting? Despite the promise of "fun," everything here was just as programmed and controlled as home.

Terry made his way back to the cabin, where his dad and mom were unpacking.

"This is a new place for us, Terry, and first impressions are important," said Bert, with one eyebrow raised. "You know what I expect of you."

Terry nodded. *Yeah. You want me to be the good little pastor's kid.*

"Yes, Dad," he replied. "I'll stay out of trouble." Like *that* was even a possibility.

He walked back to the cabin door and took a look around the camp. That restless energy was already at work.

Maybe I'll find somebody to sneak away with me for a smoke and a drink, the way Murray and I did last year in Parkside. He had snuck a few cigarettes from home, but there was no beer here. Maybe that would be the challenge—to slip away unnoticed, hike to a nearby store, and figure out how to get a six-pack.

Otherwise, baseball and monitored swimming times would have to do. *Okay*—but not exactly exciting. The challenge he needed would have to come from somewhere else.

By the end of the day, the controls had set in and it was time for the camp's feature event: a revival service in the tabernacle over by the bay.

The meetings that year featured Dwight McLaughlin, an Assemblies of God official from the northwestern U.S. A big man with silver hair and a broad smile, he struck Terry as warm and friendly, not nearly as reserved as a lot of stick-in-the-mud pastors he knew. The only bad thing was that every time McLaughlin preached he encouraged all the teenagers to answer a "call" to enter the ministry.

One evening in particular, he gave an impassioned plea for them to become missionaries.

"There's nothing in all the world more exciting than winning souls to Jesus!" he said, wearing a huge grin.

Yeah right, Terry thought, sarcastically. *Sounds like a real blast.*

"Especially over *there* where the people have *never* heard." McLaughlin thrust his finger towards the bay outside, but he was obviously pointing at something a lot more distant. And then he began to talk about Africa and India and China and a host of other unappealing places. He had preached in every country he talked about, and had even lived in Belgium at one time.

As he listened, though, Terry found himself strangely attracted by McLaughlin's descriptions. *Oh no, no, no...*he thought, shaking himself. Sure, he was bored with life—but struggling and suffering for Jesus was not in the cards. And he could smell an altar call coming—they *always* came at camp. First there would be stories of formerly wayward youth who had come to Christ and since committed their whole lives to take the gospel overseas. Then some soft music would start, and everyone would bow their heads and close their eyes. After that, he'd have everybody stand and start calling people forward.

People are going to stream to the altar, Terry thought. This guy was really good.

He was relieved that he had chosen a corner seat near the back of the big tabernacle. The only challenge he had now was how to keep from looking bored, while in the back of his mind he was figuring the best hiding place at camp to sneak a smoke when this yearly ritual was over. Maybe somewhere farther down the beach.

And yet that tiniest little stirring would not leave him alone. And without realizing it he was fighting inside.

Being a missionary was the one thing Terry had always assumed was even worse than being a pastor. There was *nobody* poorer than missionaries, and they were always dependent on everybody else for money. Plus, there was no glory or glamor in what they did.

But as McLaughlin went on, he made the world of a missionary sound as fascinating as those movies at the Orpheum, and Terry could feel himself being pulled in. The man even made *Africa* sound exciting, and he had never heard a preacher manage that!

"We often preach to big crowds out in a field, under a red African sunset," said the preacher. "And when it gets dark, they just aim a Jeep's headlights at me and we keep going."

Terry closed his eyes and felt himself being transported into the world McLaughlin was describing.

"Most times they have no musical instruments, but African choirs don't need them," McLaughlin enthused. "They grow up singing in four-part harmony and just take you right to heaven!"

In his mind's-eye, Terry could see himself preaching somewhere like that—somewhere far away and nothing like Canada.

Get a hold of yourself. That's the last thing you'd want.

"Tonight is your night," said McLaughlin, as he signaled someone to come to the piano. "*This*...is your time!"

That line was straight out of Bert Law's playbook back on Central Avenue in Prince Albert, except that McLaughlin said it like he was announcing the winner of some big contest.

In the row in front of Terry, one girl was weeping, and he knew that in another five minutes she would be crying her eyes out at the altar.

Ah, rubbish, thought Terry, shaking off the pressure he felt. *There's no way I'm going down there and committing my life to missions. Not gonna happen....*

McLaughlin had everyone stand up, with their heads bowed and eyes closed. *Cue the music*, Terry smirked to himself. *Here comes the call.*

"If you've heard the voice of God calling you tonight, it's time to answer" said McLaughlin, suddenly softer in his tone. The pianist was playing, *I'll Go Where You Want Me to Go, Dear Lord*. Terry hated that song.

"God's got a plan for your life, and somewhere in the world, someone is waiting for *you*! Step out from where you're standing and come to this altar. Let God use *you* to change the world."

Terry raised his head a little and looked around the room. Sure enough, young people were streaming to the front and kneeling.

At that moment, Terry heard a voice saying inside. *Do it.*

Come on, that's impossible, said a different voice. *You hate Africa and, besides, you can't even be a Christian at home. What makes you think God would send you anywhere?* The accusing question brought him crashing back to earth, back to reality. He'd fail if he tried to do any of the things McLaughlin was taking about. And he'd be poor, driving some clunker from church to church, begging congregations for enough money to move some place where *they* sure wouldn't want to live.

Forget it. Not gonna happen.

Terry tried to laugh the whole idea off, and started to leave, but now he *couldn't* move. A storm had begun to rage in the depths of his being. The image of himself preaching in another land was so vivid that it had paralyzed him—he was afraid to go to the altar, yet just as afraid to leave.

After the meeting, Terry sat glued to the hard two-by-twelve boards that passed for a tabernacle pew, while everyone else walked back to their cabins to get some sleep. Breakfast, and a morning meeting with McLaughlin, would come early. Thirty minutes passed, then an hour. The scene in his mind wouldn't leave him. It just kept playing, over and over. He was preaching to big crowds of people somewhere far away.

I should just get up and go walk on the beach, or go back to my room and get in bed.

But somehow he couldn't pry himself from the pew. The empty tabernacle had become the Orpheum, and he *had* walked past the stage and right into the movie, into a starring role. But it was the wrong one! He had always seen himself as James Dean's rebel without a cause—he was good at that—not one of Dwight McLaughlin's penniless missionaries.

Sometime at around 11 p.m., a caretaker failed to notice the preacher's son sitting motionless in the back of the room, and turned out the lights. Now, in total darkness, Terry could hear the wind whipping through the trees outside, as an unusually chilly rain moved into the camp from across the bay. But the storm inside him was worse than anything happening outside.

A sudden gust rattled the tabernacle door, but he hardly noticed, so trivial was it compared to the whirlwind in his soul. It howled at him from every direction, at a pitch he'd never known before. It sounded like there were voices in it: McLaughlin, Brian Albright, his parents—*be sure your sin will find you out*—voices calling to him from every direction. Even one he thought he recognized, but could not honestly say he had ever heard before. God just didn't talk to rejects like him, did he?

The door shifted again, but this time it opened and closed, and he could hear someone feeling his way along the pews, down the center aisle towards the front of the darkened hall. It was Dwight McLaughlin. He had talked and prayed with so many people at the altar that he had left his Bible lying on the pulpit, and had come to retrieve it. Terry heard the preacher pick up his book and then stop.

"Is somebody there?" asked the reverend.

"Yes, sir," Terry answered timidly, without identifying himself.

Slowly, McLaughlin felt his way back along the sawdust aisle, before shuffling sideways through the gravel between two pews. At last he stood in front of Terry, who still did not move, even when he felt a big hand touch the top of his head.

"I see you standing before a large crowd of people someday," said the man of God with quiet intensity. "You've got a Bible in your hand and you're preaching to tens of thousands of people at once. God is going to use you in foreign lands."

Terry sat still and made no reply, but inwardly he suddenly exploded, as McLaughlin's words tore through him like a tornado that rips a kitchen off its foundation while leaving the paintings in the parlor hanging in place.

This isn't happening, he told himself. *Not to me.* He was too stunned to cry, but his face was on fire, and he was glad it was dark. *Please, preacher, just leave me alone,* he pled inwardly, squeezing his closed eyes like a child making a wish. *God, just leave me alone.*

McLaughlin withdrew his hand and stood for a moment, as if waiting for a response, then sidled silently back to the aisle and out the rear door. Once again, Terry sat alone in the dark. Only now, the storm and the wind and the voices inside him had stopped. All but one.

"You're preaching to tens of thousands of people at once. God is going to use you...."

It was nearing 1 a.m. when at last Terry stepped outside and walked across the wet grass toward his family's cabin, a cold mist dampening his face and clouding his glasses. Quietly, he opened the door and tiptoed past his parents' bedroom to the one he shared with little brother, Clayton. He knew he should be sleepy, but even after he crawled into bed and pulled the covers into place, Terry lay there staring up at the ceiling, as McLaughlin's voice played over and over in his mind, wreaking havoc with all his plans. The nice clothes, the Meteor with the bullet grille, law school, his career in politics—it would all be gone before he ever had it. *You'll be stuck in a hut somewhere in Africa, wearing hand-me-downs,* he told himself. *You'll never learn to preach like your dad, and besides, what makes you think you can please God when you can't even please your parents?*

The lousy movie was still playing on the ceiling when the fog of sleep finally rolled in. Yet even then, a voice still spoke. It was softer now, and different somehow from McLaughlin's. Yet the words were unmistakably the same.

"God is going to use you."

Nine restless hours later, Terry was back in the tabernacle for the 10 a.m. service, again featuring Dwight McLaughlin. This time he sat closer to the front, but still near the wall. *Maybe he won't know which one I am,* he thought. *It was pretty dark in here last night.*

All his life to this point, Terry had felt singled out because he was a Christian and everyone expected him to excel like his father. Then came the intensity of last night's "prophecy." All he wanted was to get through the rest of camp week unnoticed and go back to being a kid with his own ideas of how his life should go.

As the preacher entered the chapel and mounted the platform, Terry slunk lower in his seat. *If I keep my head down he'll never notice me.*

"Which one of you is the young man I prayed for late last night?" asked McLaughlin, as soon as he reached the podium.

With the heat of embarrassment rising from his collar, Terry reluctantly raised his hand.

"Come up here," said McLaughlin, waving him forward with an enthusiasm that might as well have been a loaded gun. He wished he could run.

Knowing he could not refuse to cooperate, Terry rose to his feet, sheepishly excusing himself as he bumped past half a dozen pairs of knees. Walking to the front of the chapel, feeling every eye on him, he mounted the three steps onto the platform, where the big man immediately pulled him in close.

Facing the staring audience, Terry wanted to shrink.

"Last night God spoke to me about this young man," said McLaughlin. "He has a call to the nations, and I want you all to know who he is. Someday, he is going to preach the gospel to large crowds in other lands."

Terry squirmed. A calling? The proclamation hit him more like a prison sentence.

This is so ridiculous, he thought. *I could never do this stuff even if I wanted to.*

But as he rejected the idea, the picture that had formed in his mind's-eye the night before during McLaughlin's sermon arose again.

He was standing before throngs of people...preaching....

It was exactly what McLaughlin had described later when he'd found Terry sitting alone in the dark—and now he was telling everyone!

But the whole scenario was impossible, wasn't it?

There was another sense, though. Something down in the deepest part of his gut, and he thought, *Why do I want to believe it?*

After three or four minutes that felt like an eternity, the preacher released him with a pat on the shoulder. Nearly running back to his place in the crowd, Terry found a seat nearer the aisle so he could get outside quickly once the sermon was finished.

He was trembling and his face was still burning. *There's no way—no way in the world I'll ever do those things,* he told himself again. But now the vision of preaching overseas was stirring up the previous night's inner struggle. *Why won't it just leave me alone?*

Throughout the rest of his days at camp, the scene never left him....

For the rest of the year, in fact, the image hounded him, flashing over and over like lightning in his imagination. Each time, his own doubt and self-loathing thundered more loudly in response. The now-torturous vision even followed him back home to Saskatchewan that winter, when his dad accepted a pastorate in the university city of Regina.

When his senior year of high school rolled around three years later, Terry was exempted from final exams because of his consistently excellent grades. But academic achievement had not calmed his inner conflict, nor had increasing his consumption of alcohol, something he had found much easier to obtain in a larger city like Regina.

Why won't it leave me alone? he asked himself night after night, as McLaughlin's prophecy invaded his drunken stupor. *You're going to preach to large crowds...God is going to use you.*

Nothing could stop the movie, nor satisfy the hunger it had awakened in him. Constantly restless in his spirit, yet eager to feel the same stir of excitement he had felt that night, Terry began committing pranks that bordered on petty crime.

He was one of the cool kids at school now, and schoolyard bullies like Brian Albright were no longer a problem. Now, he faced bigger, tougher opponents like angry neighbors, the police and his own parents. *Especially* his parents.

The embodiment of authority, duty, success without wealth, a life of service without reward—Terry's father now represented everything he despised: He was the "godly" man who did everything right and never failed. With everything in him, he hated the fact that he could never be, and didn't want to be, like his dad.

Terry knew a confrontation was coming, and it finally arrived.

One evening, Terry and two buddies sneaked up behind a couple who were making out at the "lover's lane" on the edge of town, and used stolen garden hoses to tie their car's rear bumper to a large tree. Then, still crouching low, the boys banged loudly on the trunk of the car.

The girl screamed. The guy swore, and then impulsively started the engine, threw the car in gear and stomped on the gas.

A split-second later, as the hose stretched to its limit, there was the loud pop of metal as the car's rear bumper flew back and up, landing in the branches of the tree.

Laughing at their prank, Terry and the guys walked back into town, only to be spotted by a police cruiser that was already on alert.

Instantly, the three took off running through a nearby neighborhood, crisscrossing yards and alleys until they reached the Law's backyard, where they dove for shelter in the bushes.

For a few minutes they listened, hearing the cruiser slowly roll by, watching its searchlight scan the houses. Then it passed on.

Once they had assured themselves that the coast was clear, the other two guys took off running for home, while Terry hoisted a ladder against the house and began climbing into his second-story bedroom window. He almost made it.

One careless thump against the side of the house, and Terry had made enough noise to awaken his mother.

As it happened, Bert was attending a conference out of town, and Ann went into action to protect her family. Armed with a baseball bat, she crept down the hall and flipped on the light switch to confront the intruder, only to catch Terry half-in and half-out of the bedroom window.

When Bert arrived home a couple of days later he began to tear into his son, shouting and reading Terry the riot act. "You are grounded. You'll do exactly as I say. And you can forget hanging out with those so-called friends of yours, too. They're nothing but a bad influence."

Terry smirked in response. *We both know I'm the bad influence*, he thought.

His son's arrogant expression sent fire through Terry's dad, who, without thinking, brought his right arm up and smashed the heel of his hand into Terry's chin, knocking him over the dining room table onto the floor.

But by now, at 15 and nearly as tall as his father, Terry felt more anger than fear. In fact, he no longer feared his dad at all.

Quickly regaining his feet, he stood up and stuck out his chin.

"Go ahead. Hit me again."

Bert Law froze. And the second blow never came. Instead, with a wave of his hand, he turned his back, disgusted. "I give up. I can't do anything with you."

As far as Terry was concerned, it might as well have been the voice of God. *I can't do anything with you.* Wasn't that what he had always expected? And isn't that what he wanted—to be left alone?

Walking back upstairs to his room, Terry wore a defiant grin. His jaw ached, but it had been worth it to face down his dad. In the span of three days he had defeated his two biggest foes—the police and his father—once and for all.

You're finally your own man, Terry Law, he congratulated himself. Yet somehow the boast rang hollow instead of thrilling, and if anything, he found himself becoming even angrier than before. Defying authority, even winning the battle with his dad, wasn't enough. He needed something more stimulating, more daring. Something dangerous... even explosive.

It wasn't really that hard to persuade a couple of classmates to steal bomb-making ingredients from Central High School's science lab. Neil, a lanky blond with a genius for chemistry, was reeled in more by scientific curiosity than a desire to break the law. Murray, a toothy, freckled redhead, was easily swayed by any promise of adventure, especially the kind old timers at reunions reminisce about as their "crazy high school days."

Assembling the device was risky. First, they had to steal a sufficient amount of a highly volatile white powder called potassium chlorate from chemistry class, along with enough hydro-sulfuric acid to set it off. Then Murray, who quickly built a secret lab in his parents' basement, would carefully load the powder into a 30-inch length of heavy plumber's pipe that was sealed on one end. Terry, whose newfound thirst for danger was growing stronger by the day, would place and detonate the bomb. Of course, the textbook in whose pages they found the recipe had borne the requisite warning of explosion, but to the three sixteen-year old rowdies it constituted an invitation.

It was a frosty night in November when the trio combed north Regina, until they found a sleepy neighborhood whose back alley was rich with targets: a long line of outdoor toilets, which, in 1959, were still a common household necessity.

Neil parked his dad's bright yellow Plymouth Fury on a nearby street, and quietly the three began tiptoeing their way along the alley, searching for the ideal structure. Neil and Murray skulked along the line of chain-link fences, while Terry, holding the open end of the pipe upright at arm's length, took more deliberate steps. He looked for all the world like a color bearer who had lost his flag.

"There it is," said Terry in a hoarse whisper. "That one's perfect!"

"It" was a two-door unit, well constructed and anchored to a concrete slab. Without doubt the finest privy in the neighborhood, it was indeed a "high-value" target. But such perfection came with a risk: just thirty feet separated the little shed from the back door of the house, whose lights were on. At any moment someone inside could walk out and catch them in the act. Worse, lives could be lost.

Reality dawned on Neil and Murray, who began giggling nervously at the danger.

"Let's get out of here!" they whispered to each other, and then sprinted back down the alley to the yellow Plymouth, practically diving into the front seat when they got there. Neil cranked the engine, ready to pull away as soon as Terry slid in back. But the angry preacher's son had stayed behind to finish the job.

There's no way you're stopping now, Law, he told himself as he opened the toilet's door. A single squeak might give him away.

Once inside the two-stall structure Terry worked quickly but cautiously, leaning the bomb upright against the middle partition.

Do your job right, Terry, he instructed himself as he inserted a small metal funnel into the pipe's opening, and then stuffed it with the toilet tissue that lay nearby.

Pack it tight...more, a little more. If that acid soaks through too quickly you're a dead man.

Terry drew the small beaker of hydro-sulfuric acid from his pocket and poured it onto the tissue. "Calm and steady," he whispered, as he tried his best not to imagine himself being blown to bits at any moment. "There, that's enough."

In a single, fluid movement, Terry set the beaker down with one hand and opened the wooden door with the other. Then he dashed outside, through the gate and down the alley with the speed of an Olympic runner.

Reaching the car, he stood by its open rear door for a moment and peered back at the darkness. *Why is there no explosion?* he wondered.

"It's not going to work," said Murray. But no sooner had the words left his lips than a huge fireball billowed upward in the distance, followed by a tremendous *boom* that shook both the car and the ground beneath it.

Suddenly bits of wood and paper, human waste, and fetid water began raining from the sky, the flotsam and feces landing on the roofs of cars and houses, smearing walls and windows.

"Holy cow!" shrieked Murray, as Neil jerked the Plymouth into gear and Terry ducked inside, trying to muffle a string of giddy curses.

Less than a minute later they were rumbling southward along the main boulevard in a getaway as loud as the Plymouth's paint job.

Elated as they were by their success, the boys were even more thrilled by the next morning's lead story in the Regina *Leader Post*. The chief of police himself had written it, pronouncing the caper "the worst crime of the night."

For days following, Terry was gripped by a nearly unbearable urge to do it again, to set off a bigger, more powerful bomb. The memory of the fireball mushrooming above the houses and trees—that moment had given him the biggest adrenalin rush of his life, even bigger than McLaughlin's stupid "vision" of him preaching somewhere in Africa.

Finally, Terry could contain himself no longer. "Why not build a bigger one?" he asked his accomplices.

Neil wasn't sure he wanted to go along—the sight of that fireball had drained his courage. But Murray grinned and quickly agreed to start looking for a new formula.

"As soon as you find something, we'll meet in your basement and figure out what we want to blow up next," said Terry.

Within days, Murray said he had found the key ingredient for a more powerful device—something called picric acid—and the three agreed to meet right away.

A couple of evenings later, Terry and Neil were on their way to Murray's house when they walked past a pool hall. It was a seedy joint, but one where they knew the owner would admit underage boys. Three games and a few beers later, the two realized they probably were no longer sharp enough to handle something as dangerous as picric acid. The stuff was not only more volatile than potassium chlorate but also more unstable, especially if it began to dry. It could even form explosive salts when its residue rubbed against storage lids or concrete. And, of course, Murray's lab was located in a concrete basement, a fact that convinced even Terry that they should just call it a night and go home. By midnight, both were at home and asleep in their beds.

The alarm clock hadn't yet sounded the next morning when Terry's mom awakened him to say that Neil was on the phone, and that he sounded upset. Groggy, Terry crawled out of bed and walked downstairs to pick up the receiver.

"Have you listened to the news?" asked Neil.

"No," replied Terry, suddenly shaken awake by the fear in Neil's voice.

"Murray's basement blew up last night...He's dead!" exclaimed Neil, nearly in tears. "What are we going to do? He's dead, Terry—dead!"

Terry was instantly sick, and for a moment he couldn't speak. "There's nothing we can do, Neil," he finally managed. "Let's just get dressed and go to school."

Central High School's usually noisy hallways were quiet that morning, except for the sounds of whispers and muffled tears.

"Have you heard...?" a couple of students started to ask Terry, but the ashen look on his face gave them their answer before they could finish.

I should be dead, he thought as he opened his locker. The horrid fact punched him in the stomach and he almost vomited. *Neil and I should both be dead. If we hadn't decided to play pool at the last minute. If we hadn't been drinking....*

Three days later, as he stood by a grave, helping to lower the charred remains of the late Murray Ingham into the ground, Terry once again heard the voice from Nanoose Bay. This time, however, it spoke not of his future, but of the awful present he could not escape.

You said nothing. You never told Murray one word about Jesus, and now it's too late.

The voice spoke in tones neither of hope nor accusation, but with sorrow. And for the first time in his life, Terry felt remorse. The kind that wounds you in the heart, and carves a hole in your spirit that can never be—and by God's grace *shouldn't be*—healed.

Then he remembered a verse in the *Book of Romans* that says, God works all things together for good for "those who are called according to his purpose."

For those who are called. That's me, he thought, wiping away hot, bitter tears. *God called me, and I wouldn't answer. No more chances. Now it's too late.*

As he left the cemetery on that chilly spring day in 1960, utterly blinded by his failure, Terry could not possibly have seen how anything good might ever come from Murray's death. Instead, all he saw was his friend's face, staring at him from somewhere far, far away. He couldn't tell where, but he had an idea it wasn't heaven.

In place of the toothy, mischievous grin, Murray was wearing a tragic, puzzled stare. One that was asking, over and over, *Why didn't you say something?*

For weeks, then months, Murray's face haunted Terry day and night, and he wondered if it would ever go away. How desperately he hoped it would!

But how fortunate for him, and for the souls of those that would someday stand before him all over the world, that his late friend's troubling image would not go away. For there would come a day much later, when Terry would realize that Murray's death, by God's mysterious grace, had led to *his* resurrection, and that his inner storms had not been calmed by command, but by surrender. Then and only then, with the skies of his soul finally made clear, could he begin to glimpse the grand adventure of a life lived for God's purposes.

For now, though, neither the face of Murray Ingham nor the voice of God would leave him alone.

CHAPTER 3

FIRST LIGHT

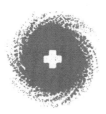

FOR THE REST of his senior year of high school, Terry was racked
with guilt, not only over Murray's death but also by the fact that
somehow *he* had survived.

Why me—why did God allow me to live? he asked himself over
and over, until the question had distilled itself into a much more
basic one:

Why am I alive in the first place?

Hadn't he heard that question all his life at church, his dad's
street meetings and every summer at camp? Wasn't it the one
Dwight McLaughlin had awakened in him at Nanoose Bay?

Yes, but McLaughlin had also *answered* it, and that was what
had made his life since Murray's death so miserable. Until he had
seen the electrifying vision of himself preaching to multitudes in
far-off lands, Terry had lived in a little religious pond, surrounded
by a big fence that posted the limits of "good" Christian behavior.
But McLaughlin had torn the fence down, opening up a world of
possibilities that were fascinating but also unknown and scary.

Now, Terry realized that his continual displays of bravado—
defying the police, building bombs, and daring his dad to "hit

me again"—had only laid bare the truth. He wasn't brave, but afraid—afraid of God, whom he had always thought looked only at his sins. Afraid of what God might require of him and where he might send him. Afraid of failing if he answered that calling.

Unwilling to obey what he could no longer deny, Terry began drinking more and more heavily. By the time he started law school at the University of Saskatchewan in the fall, he could feel himself spiritually and mentally nearing a sort of negative critical mass.

The tipping point came on the Sunday following his first week of classes, when Terry and two friends drank the afternoon away and then decided to go to his dad's church, where a guest evangelist was scheduled to speak.

"We'll wait until the music is finished and this guy starts preaching," he had told them. "Then we'll raise a ruckus my dad will never forget! Just wait for my signal."

The three made their entrance as the last hymn was winding up. *This is going to be fun*, Terry told himself. The beer had been good, and he felt ready. It was just a matter of picking the right time to make the maximum impact.

But the right moment never came. Instead, as the preacher spoke, Terry began sobering up—far more quickly, in fact, than he should have, given how much beer he had drunk.

What's happening to me? he asked himself. *This guy's not even that good a preacher.*

On and on, the evangelist droned, but the longer he talked the more aware Terry became that something powerful was overtaking him, pulling him out of his stupor to get his attention. Anger at his parents, resentment of his religion, remorse for Murray's death, the restless feeling that had driven him to ridiculous extremes—all the horrible emotions the beer had failed to deaden were suddenly staring him in the face. There was no more putting it off. He had to deal with them now.

Terry glanced over at his bleary-eyed co-conspirators, still awaiting his nod, and he realized he no longer wanted to carry out his plan. He knew they would tease him later for losing his nerve, but he was beginning to not care what they thought. "Blah, blah, blah," the preacher seemed to be saying. But it might as well have been the greatest sermon ever preached.

Terry felt his mind tilting back and forth—*I've gone too far with my own plans to turn back now...I need to do what God wants me to do*—like two storm winds rising and clashing in his soul.

You can't take anymore of this, a voice whispered in his heart. Terry winced. The voice from Nanoose Bay was back, quiet and gentle, and without competition. There was no explosion this time, and no urge to run away.

I give up. I'm done with running away, Terry told himself, as hot tears began trailing down his cheeks. A lifetime of anger seemed to be draining out of him.

Is there a reason you kept me from going to Murray's house that night? Is this why I lived—to actually make a difference in the world? How could you possibly want a kid like me?

At once, McLaughlin's prophecy that had played so relentlessly in the back of Terry's thoughts for the past three years was front and center in his mind's-eye. He was preaching to somebody—he didn't know whom—somewhere on the other side of the world.

How could such a thing be possible? He had been running *away* from God much of his life. He didn't want to live the life of a poor, struggling missionary.

Terry shifted in his seat. He could feel his feet wanting to move.

"In conclusion..." said the preacher.

Terry agonized. He knew what was coming next and he couldn't wait to get it over with.

At last, the evangelist stopped his rambling and commenced the liturgy that every lifelong Pentecostal knew by heart.

"Every head bowed and every eye closed," he recited, as the congregation rose to their feet and someone at the piano began to play. "If you're ready to turn your life over to Jesus, just step out and..."

Before the sentence was halfway spoken, Terry found himself moving...almost bolting for the altar, leaving his buddies slack-jawed on the back row.

"Dear God, I'll do it," he vowed as his elbows crashed against the altar rail...and then his years of resistance collapsed into a flood of pent-up tears. "I'll go anywhere and do anything. Africa, China—I don't care anymore. I'll go."

The vision before him was fully unfolding now. He was preaching to people somewhere on the other side of the world— people caught in the storms of life. He didn't care how far it was or what it might cost him. All he knew was that he wanted to be there.

"McLaughlin was right, Lord," he sobbed quietly. "They're out there waiting for help."

All his life, Terry had heard about the suffering masses in other countries. Children in Africa who lacked food and shelter. Victims of injustice and war in the Middle East. Christians in communist countries who were persecuted just for being Christians. But now, as though through a fog, he was beginning to *see* them.

For thirty minutes—or was it an hour?—he leaned against an altar rail that, for now, had become his own window on the world. He saw the crowds McLaughlin had described, hundreds of thousands of faces—millions, maybe—of so many different colors. And in what seemed like a hundred different languages, they were lifting their voices in praise to the God who loved them—who loved *him*.

"Oh, God, I'm so sorry for..." he whispered, but before he could begin reciting his list of regrets he knew they no longer mattered.

So this is what grace is. It was never about a bunch of rules—never about being worthy or earning your love. I don't have to earn anything.

He opened his mouth again, but his speech failed him.

Why me, God? Why? he groaned within. *How could you love me? I know you love all those suffering people who've never heard of Jesus, but I've got no excuse. I fought against you so hard and failed every promise I ever made to you.*

At last, Terry opened his eyes and looked around. The congregation was gone, and he saw his dad standing nearby, quietly waiting to lock the building. Without speaking, he wiped his eyes and stood to his feet.

"God, I promise you this," he vowed without moving his lips. "For as long as I live, there will never be another Murray Ingham in my life, never another soul that I fail to tell about you."

Bert and Ann Law were quiet that night when their son came downstairs from his room and dropped down on the living-room sofa, his eyes still red behind his glasses. Terry looked over at his younger sister, Lois, who wore an expression of wry skepticism.

I really can't blame you, he thought. He knew she had seen this act before, and that he usually fell off his emotional mountains as quickly as he climbed them.

Then he looked at his father.

"Dad, I'm not fighting my call to preach any longer," he said meekly. "I need to get my money back from the university and enroll at Bethel Bible Institute, where you and Mom went."

Terry's parents looked at one another, their faces flickering with cautious optimism. Like Lois, they knew from years past that Terry could rescind declarations as rashly as he made them. And so far their hopes had been dashed every time.

"Son, you paid your tuition and you've been in class for a week already," replied Bert calmly, trying to temper the joy bubbling up in his spirit. "That law school isn't obligated to refund a single penny. I doubt if they'll agree."

"I know, Dad, but if God has really called me then he's going to make a way," Terry insisted. "I'll go and see the dean first thing tomorrow morning and try to get a refund."

The sun had barely risen on Monday morning when Terry walked into the administration building at the University of Saskatchewan to plead his case.

"I need to ask a big favor from you, sir," he said to the Dean of Students, who sat behind his massive mahogany desk. Terry had rehearsed his request a dozen different ways during the drive from home, and every one had sounded as ridiculous as the last.

Might as well just come straight to the point.

"I know this sounds crazy, but last night God changed my life, and I have come to realize that I'm supposed to travel the world preaching the gospel instead of going into law."

You're right, Law. This does sound crazy, he thought as the dean raised his eyebrows in a look of total surprise.

"I've been fighting this since I was fourteen, but I just can't get away from it. I don't know how, but I know I'm called to be a preacher, not a lawyer."

The dean stared at his young freshman, then lowered his eyes and brought both hands to rest on his desk for a moment before looking up again. His expression had returned to normal, and he looked surprisingly calm.

"I have never had a request like this, Mr. Law," he said in a deep, scholarly-sounding voice. "Your tuition has already been paid in full, and I'm sure you know that if you drop out this university owes you nothing."

A dropout, thought Terry. *That's how he sees me. I'm a dropout. Oh Lord, I'm sunk.*

Terry opened his mouth and started to explain himself again, but the dean wasn't finished.

"However, I'm impressed by your honesty, Mr. Law. And you sound truly convinced that this is the right course of action for your life."

An hour later Terry placed a check for a little over $400 in his pocket, shook hands with the dean, and for the last time, walked across the campus of his former *alma mater* to his car. Two days later, his father drove him three hours north to Saskatoon, where he enrolled as a freshman at Bethel Bible Institute.

After giving Terry a two-minute tour of the dormitory he had helped build twenty-eight years earlier, Bert walked his son to his new room and extended his hand.

"Study hard and stay well, son," he said. "We'll see you in a few weeks."

Terry knew this was as close as his dad could come to congratulating him, but it was okay. *I'm finally going to make you proud of me,* he thought, as he peered through the window and watched his father drive away.

Then he turned and took a deep breath as he climbed up onto his squeaky bunk.

You're really here, Terry. You're going to get straight A's, spend time in prayer, and learn to preach. Then you're going to take the gospel wherever God calls you, no matter what.

Terry was surprised with himself for thinking so boldly. Not that he wasn't accustomed to bold thoughts—he just wasn't used to thinking *constructive* ones. Getting into trouble had always come easily to him, especially compared to all those "perfect" kids he knew from camp, most of whom were now well on their way to becoming pastors and missionaries. Some of whom he had already passed in the hallway here at Bethel. He wondered how he would manage to fit in.

Well, at least you finally know God doesn't call perfect people, he reassured himself. *Now just take the bull by the horns and do a good job.*

For the first time in his seventeen years, Terry Law was realizing the true simplicity of living the Christian life: Keeping the rules is not the point, nor is figuring out some way to earn God's love. Instead, it's all about surrender, and knowing that when God calls you, he's also going to make that calling come to pass.

Terry looked about the room and bounced himself gently a couple of times to test the squeaks in his bed. After years of struggling with self-condemnation, he felt truly carefree.

Then he noticed a large white envelope lying on his pillow.

CHAPTER 4

THE DESERT

STARTING TO FEEL AT HOME in a dorm room his dad had helped build nearly three decades earlier, Terry opened the packet someone had placed on his pillow. It was labeled *New Students*.

"Welcome to Bethel Bible Institute!" the form letter began. Terry quickly skimmed the rest of the page and turned to the next one. "CODE OF CONDUCT," it said, in centered caps across the top.

> 1. *No consumption of alcoholic drinks. Violation will result in immediate expulsion.*

Yeah, no problem, he told himself. He hadn't even *wanted* a drink since last Sunday night at the altar. He kept reading.

> 2. *No use of tobacco products in any form. Violation will result in revocation of privileges.*

No surprise there either, he thought, although giving up cigarettes was something he hadn't yet managed to do.

Number 3 forbade movies and number 4 dealt with dancing. Terry had expected each rule, but not the harshly worded penalties attached to them. He began to feel cold inside. What had he done?

Is this you, God, or am I really still that unspiritual? he wondered.

No lipstick allowed...no shorts or women's slacks...curfew at 10 p.m....no chewing gum during chapel service....

Terry's eyes raced down the page, and by the time he reached the bottom, he was craving a cigarette.

"Continued on page 3..."

What?

"What in the world have you gotten yourself into?" he wondered out loud, as the smile left his face.

It rarely reappeared for the next twenty months. Being Bethel's version of a "good" Christian seemed impossible. Month after month, he was either being praised for his straight-A average or threatened with expulsion. And worse than the endless list of prohibitions, he hated the ten o'clock curfew that made him feel so hemmed in.

By the beginning of his second year at Bethel Terry was smoking more than ever, a sure sign he was a spiritual failure, even by his own standards. He had never felt so confined—so trapped—in his whole life. He was back in the pond, surrounded by a bigger fence than ever. Other than a third year's tuition to Bethel, he had no money, no job, no car, and no way out, other than a remote possibility he had heard about a few days earlier.

The King's Men, a good gospel quartet from Northwest Bible College up in Edmonton, was rumored to be in the market for a bass singer.

At least it's worth a phone call, thought Terry, as he cobbled together a handful of change and headed for a phone booth not far from campus.

"Hi, this is Terry Law. I'm a student down at Bethel."

Use your best speaking voice, Terry, he reminded himself.

"I hear that your group might be looking for a bass singer. I'd like to come up and audition, and maybe take a look at the college while I'm there."

"Can you preach?" asked John Martz, the group's leader.

"Uh, yes sir. That's what I've been training to do for the past two years," said Terry.

"Great. Come on up and we'll meet next Friday night," replied John.

A week later, Terry was the future bass singer of the King's Men quartet. A month later he was Northwest Bible College's newest enrollee.

"Northwest has a more international perspective," he told his surprised parents that summer, explaining that the school frequently invited missionaries to speak during Sunday night chapel services. "Plus, I'll get to live with a family instead of staying in a dorm, and I'll have enough time to work a part-time job."

And no more petty rules and curfews, he rejoiced inwardly.

Unlike his time at Bethel, life at Northwest was everything Terry had hoped it would be. His classes were challenging, and on weekends he sharpened his preaching skills with the King's Men. He especially loved hearing various international speakers at Central Tabernacle, the large PAOC church that housed the school. Sure, there were inevitable appeals for money after missionaries spoke, because they badly needed it. But now these people were heroes in his eyes, not beggars.

"Who can give $100 in tonight's offering?" challenged Pastor Bob Taitinger one snowy Sunday evening that winter. "He wants to go back to Africa for another four years if we're willing to send him!"

Who's going to go first? Terry wondered, as he leaned over the balcony rail and scanned the congregation below. He knew where the "money" sat.

C'mon somebody! he thought. *This guy wants to go serve God. Lord knows, I'd do it myself if I had more than 103 bucks....*

Suddenly he felt heat rising from his collar and rushing straight to his face.

Then you could give a hundred, couldn't you? said an inner voice he had gradually come to recognize.

Lord, that would only leave me with three dollars to my name, he objected, thinking at once of the subzero weather outside. *I'll run out of bus money and spend the rest of the winter wading six miles through the snow each day.*

Trust me and do it anyway, said the voice.

I'll just raise my hand a little, and if the pastor doesn't see me the first time, I won't raise it again, he reasoned.

"Yes, I see that hand. Thank you, Terry!" said the pastor as soon as his fingertips cleared the balcony rail.

Three days later, on Wednesday morning, Terry handed his last few coins to the bus driver and rode to school. It was twenty degrees below zero when his final class ended that afternoon, and he dreaded the long walk home.

Might as well go the chapel and pray a while, he told himself. His prayer life always improved a little when things went wrong.

"Lord, I did what you said," he whispered, "or at least I think it was you. But I don't know exactly what you want me to learn from it, unless it's learning how to suffer."

Terry thought about the long walk home, and decided he wanted to get it over with. He started to push himself up from the altar rail, but hesitated.

Stay a little longer.

He had stopped praying now and was just kneeling there, bracing himself for the cold, when he felt a coat sleeve brush against his shoulder. He opened his eyes and started to look up, but a sealed envelope lying on the altar in front of him caught his eye instead. Behind him, he heard the chapel door open and close.

Still on his knees, he picked up the envelope. It was fat. *Someone must have written me a letter*, he thought, as he slowly broke the seal and reached inside. Instead of a letter, there was money. Paper money.

Twenty, forty...fifty, fifty-one, fifty-two...fifty-three dollars. I've got fifty-three dollars! God, you did it—you came through!

Terry jumped to his feet and rushed out into the freezing weather to look for his benefactor, but seeing no one familiar, he headed for the bus stop. It might as well have been a warm spring day, for all the joy he felt. Now, he not only had enough money to make it through the week, but also to buy a bus ticket to his parents' new home in Medicine Hat, Alberta, where Bert had asked him to preach both Sunday sermons at his new church.

After the Sunday evening service, Terry relaxed in his parents' living room. He could tell by their cheery mood that they were pleased with his preaching, and although they had not paid him any outright compliments, his mom had baked his favorite dessert: apple pie *a la mode.*

This sure is a long way from "be sure your sins will find you out," Terry laughed inwardly as he sat down at the kitchen table to dig in.

He was about to go for a second piece when there was knock on the front door.

"Son, there's someone here to see you," called his father from the living room.

Who could it be? Terry wondered, as he got up from the table. *Everybody here is new to me.*

When he entered the living room, a slender gentleman with a broad smile, brown leathery face, and black bushy eyebrows was standing just inside the door.

"Son, this is Ed Stahl," said Bert, as the two men shook hands. "He owns a cattle ranch about fifty miles east of here, and this is his home church."

"Pleased to meet you, sir," said Terry.

"Pleased to meet you as well, young man," replied Ed. "Thank you for your messages today. I was stirred while you were speaking tonight, and felt impressed to give you this."

Ed reached into his coat pocket, pulled something out, and extended his hand. There were three $100 bills fanned across his fingers.

Terry stared at the money and tried to offer a reply.

"I...uh, I..."

"I also want you to know that when school's finished, I'll have a summer job ready for you on my ranch," Ed continued.

"Wha...really?" stammered Terry with a chuckle in his voice that made it come out, "ree-hee-heel-ee." But he couldn't help himself. This was the faithfulness of God on display, right in front of him. A week ago tonight he had given his last $100 to a missionary, only to receive nearly four times as much *plus* a job offer in return.

"Wow—Praise the Lord!" he exclaimed. "Yes, sir, I'll be more than happy to take that job as soon as school's over. Thank you, Ed. Thank you so much!"

After more handshaking, and some shoulder slapping by Bert, Ed Stahl took his leave and Terry returned to the kitchen table. He started chuckling again.

"Dad, you're not going to believe what's happened to me this week..."

After graduating with honors from Northwest the next spring, Terry hooked up with his childhood buddy, Dennis Bjorgan, to launch his own group, The Gospel Sons of Canada. Making good music and preaching in the big cities from Vancouver to Toronto for the next year and a half was more stimulating than anything he had ever done, yet nothing compared to the excitement of boarding a Norwegian freighter in Montreal with Dennis and spending a whole month crashing waves across the Atlantic to get to Capetown, South Africa.

Far from being the place of spiritual exile Terry had always imagined, Africa was every bit as exciting as Dwight McLaughlin's sermons had made it sound. At last the faces he had only seen in clouded prayer stood in plain sight before him. Maybe the crowds were not as large as McLaughlin had prophesied, but there were plenty of them, and thousands of South Africans of every color committed their lives to God.

This was *real* living, thought Terry, and even when the time came to return home the next year, he didn't mind, so sure was he that Medicine Hat was just a layover on the longer journey to his true destiny.

It was mid-summer 1966 when Terry's folks met him at the airport in Calgary, and soon he was assisting his dad with the church and working on Ed Stahl's ranch for a second time. It wouldn't be long, he told himself, until his next breakthrough came. Then he'd be off preaching again in Africa or somewhere else in God's big world. Yet as the months ticked by, no direction came, and other than the occasional invitation to speak somewhere that always seemed too much like home, Terry began to feel stymied.

Having finally gotten some real experience under his belt in Africa—the very place he used to fear—only made his present situation worse. Dressing like the Beatles while he and Dennis sang and played guitars had drawn legions of teenagers to hear them, and the memory of seeing so many kids commit their lives to Christ when he preached still gave Terry chills. But even more exciting had been the night when they had had to outrun an angry mob.

It still felt like yesterday. He and Dennis had finished an evening meeting and were leaving a South African ghetto, when a gang armed with knives and broken bottles had blocked the street in front of their car. Terry had seen the gas cans and the pile of burning tires and knew what they meant. The gang intended to "necklace" them, to shove two of the tires down over his and Dennis' shoulders, douse them in gasoline, and burn them alive. But, at the last moment they had discovered an unblocked side street and escaped.

It had been the most frightening night of his life, but also the most exciting. And somehow it made the wide open spaces of western Canada that he'd loved as a kid seem small and suffocating.

Is this it for me, God? he wondered. *Working with a youth group on Sundays and fixing holes in cattle fences the rest of the week? Is this how I'm going to spend the rest my life?*

He thought about his work with Ed. At least there were a few positives to that. Working on the ranch the first time had been hard, sweaty fun and a great change of pace from his studies. And on this second go-round he seemed to be learning as much about serving God from Ed as he had in three years of Bible school. The old rancher fascinated him, especially with his astounding ability to find water sources out on the prairie.

Terry laughed when he remembered the research team some big university had recently sent to interview Ed.

"What's your secret for finding underground springs out here on the prairie, Mr. Stahl?" the head of the team had asked.

"Oh, I just ask God to show me where to dig and he tells me the right spot every time," Ed had replied with the innocence of a child.

"You mean you're a diviner?" the professor had asked.

"Nope. I just pray and God tells me," Ed had answered.

The professors had left the ranch that day as puzzled and un-informed as when they had arrived. Terry remembered feeling embarrassed for his boss, and skeptical enough that Ed had noticed.

"Get in the truck and come with me," Ed had told him a day or two later. "I'm going to show you how to find water where there isn't any."

They had driven a few miles across the prairie, and Ed had parked his pickup at a big, barren spot of land. *No way there's water around here*, thought Terry, as he got out of the truck.

"Go dig a hole about three feet deep over there and put this bundle of dynamite in it and cover everything but the fuse," the rancher said. "Then light it and run."

The chance to blow something up had been fun, thought Terry, although he still felt a little guilty for enjoying it, considering his wayward past.

The blast had formed a crater almost big enough to park Ed's pickup inside, but the hole was still bone dry.

"Stick another bundle in there and climb out fast," Ed had instructed him.

Terry jumped in the hole, dug more dirt, placed the load, and lit the fuse. Remembering the luminous orange cloud from the bomb he'd built years earlier, he bounded out of the crater and ran away as hard and fast as he could.

It was a good thing he had moved so quickly. The second round of explosives had doubled the crater's size, sending up a red cloud of boulders and pulverized clay as big as the fiery mushroom that had nearly killed him back in Regina.

Even now, months later, Terry marveled at the memory of seeing those first muddy bubbles, surging up through the cracks in the clay. Within an hour, there had been a pond big enough to water Ed's cattle for years to come.

Terry thought about how he and Ed had repeated the process several more times that summer and hit a gusher every time. That rancher sure knew how to hear from God.

"Lord, that's what I need," Terry whispered. "I want to learn to hear your voice the way Ed does."

Little did Terry know that even then, like a fountain hidden beneath the dry desert floor, the answer to his prayer lay near, unseen but already flowing, waiting to burst upon him. But to find it, he would need to learn to run toward the explosion, right into the mushroom cloud. And not just now, but every time.

Whether fire or water, sand or storm, running *toward* the clouds in his life would be the key to his future. Because that is where God's power is greatest. That is where he reigns.

Ed Stahl's obvious sensitivity to God's voice stirred a hunger in Terry's heart that quickly turned to desperation. He knew he needed to know God—*had* to know him—the way Ed did, and now he had to take some kind of action, but what?

What do you do when it feels like you've been sidelined from the vision you thought was God? What do you do when the dream inside you feels like it will never come true?

Terry knew he couldn't go back to Africa and start up again with Dennis. His friend had come home to attend Bible school and marry his sweetheart, Cherie. But he also couldn't just spend the rest of his life here in the Hat, swimming lap after meaningless lap around the little Pentecostal pond he had grown up in.

Maybe I should set aside a few days to fast and pray, he thought. Prayer had seemed pointless to him years ago, really nothing more than reading a few verses of Scripture and asking God to "help me make it a little longer 'til Jesus comes."

But lately Terry had discovered a collection of short books on faith, written by a preacher named Kenneth Hagin, down in Oklahoma. He was impressed by Hagin's teaching that Christians should "agree with God's word by speaking it over your situation." And now, the idea of praying with purpose, with the real expectation of something good instead of just "hoping for the best," lit a fire in him.

That's it! Terry decided. *I'm going to fast and pray as long as it takes, until I hear from the Lord as clearly as Ed does on the ranch.*

"I need to spend a few days somewhere in prayer and fasting," Terry told his dad the next day. "I've got to learn to hear from God the way Ed Stahl hears him. I'm going to go crazy if I don't get some direction soon."

"Well, one of the families at church is going south to the States on vacation this week," replied Bert. "Why don't you ask them about staying at their place?"

The family quickly agreed to Terry's request and within days he had moved in and was parked on his knees in their living room, with his Bible spread open in front of him on the coffee table, and a stack of Kenneth Hagin's books nearby. He had decided to eat nothing and drink only water for the next week. That would have seemed impossible in the past, but now he was so desperate that he had lost his appetite. Hagin claimed that God would speak to Christians through his word, and at this moment that was the only thing that mattered.

Terry remembered reading in one of the books that he should personalize the Scriptures and "quote God's word after him." He looked down at his Bible and began to pray.

"Lord, you said in Proverbs 3, verses 5 and 6, that I should trust in the Lord with all my heart and lean not on my own understanding. I do trust you. And in all my ways I acknowledge you, and you shall direct my paths.

"I believe this God. I believe you will direct my paths. Not just my path, but my paths—all of them."

He grabbed the ribbon in his Bible and flipped to another passage.

"And in First Corinthians you said, 'Eye has not seen, nor ear heard, nor have entered into my heart the things which you have prepared for those who love you. But you have revealed them to me through your Spirit. For your spirit searches all things, yes, the deep things of God.'"

Be specific, Terry, he reminded himself.

"I believe that too, Lord. I believe you have revealed these things in my spirit. Not you *will* reveal them, but you *have* revealed them down in my spirit."

He remembered another passage where St. Paul had talked about praying with his spirit while his understanding remained "unfruitful."

"Lord, I know these things are down in my spirit, but I need to have them in my understanding. I'm asking you to make my mind fruitful."

He turned back to the verses in Proverbs and put his finger on the first passage he had prayed.

"Direct my paths, Lord. It's your promise right here, and I'm asking you to do it for me."

Back and forth, he turned from one set of verses to the other, and prayed them aloud until he had memorized both. Then he rose from his knees and paced the living room floor, repeating his plea.

Day became night and then day again, and he slept when he needed, without regard to clocks.

"Lord, you said in Proverbs 3, verses 5 and 6..."

Word for word, he repeated the prayer over and over, sometimes pacing, sometimes tracing the page with his finger. From Proverbs to First Corinthians, back and forth, again and again, he prayed, consulting other Scriptures as well, but always coming back to where he had begun.

"Father, you said in Isaiah 54 that 'no weapon formed against me shall prosper.' I believe you Father. You kept Dennis and me safe from the mob that night in South Africa. You directed our paths, just like Proverbs says."

The memory electrified him yet again.

"Lord, I'm willing to go back," he prayed passionately. "Men like that need to know you, and I'm willing to go and preach to them, even if it means not making it out alive. I don't care—I just need you to direct my paths again."

Seven days and seven nights came to an end, and when he packed his bags and drove back to his parents' home, Terry had still "heard" nothing. But he wasn't giving up. Not now that prayer was something more than wishful thinking.

Day after day all summer, while he toiled under a hot sun on Ed's ranch, Terry recited exactly what the Bible said about *him*, that God would direct his paths to the right places—he knew it was somewhere overseas—where lost souls were waiting to hear him tell them about God. Whether the people in those distant lands knew it or not was beside the point now. They were out there waiting for someone, and that someone was him.

You know where, God, he repeated over and over while he dug holes, hauled bales and fed cattle. *And sooner or later, I'll know too.*

Sooner, in fact, rather than later, Terry would learn exactly where he must go in following God. But first, he just needed to know God himself. Because it is the *sound* of the Shepherd's voice, not merely a set of directions, that his sheep must learn to follow.

CHAPTER 5

TRAINING DAY

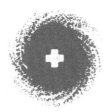

IT WAS EARLY AUGUST when Terry asked Ed for a day off from the ranch to drive to Edmonton to hear Oral Roberts, the famous healing evangelist from Tulsa, Oklahoma.

"I'd like to attend one of the crusade services at the hockey arena," said Terry.

"No problem," Ed replied without hesitation. "Take the whole day. You'll need to leave early to get a good seat."

Terry hit the road the next morning, and used the long drive to Edmonton to mull over his future. He tried his best to stay positive and let his dreams grow, but in the back of his mind one question kept teasing him.

How are you ever going to pull off an overseas ministry when you barely make enough money to make ends meet? Look at where you are, out here in the middle of the prairie. Face it: You're nobody special, and it's not like you have many contacts.

He pushed the doubts out of his mind, intent only on seeing Oral Roberts preach. Maybe he could learn something from Roberts' speaking style and how he held his crusades.

When he arrived at the arena that afternoon it was empty,

except for Roberts' musicians, who were rehearsing for the evening's service.

The organist looked like he was in his early twenties, but his playing was phenomenal. Terry took a seat on the front row, as close to the stage as he could get. This guy was easily the best musician he had ever heard.

As soon as the band took a break, Terry walked to the steps at the edge of the stage to introduce himself.

"Hi, I'm an evangelist from Medicine Hat," Terry said as the two shook hands. *Man, I sound like a country boy*, he thought, and quickly added, "I recently spent a year touring and preaching in South Africa. Right now I'm assisting my dad at his church."

"Larry Dalton. Pleased to meet you."

This guy's hands are huge, Terry said to himself. *No wonder he can play like that.*

"I'm from Big Stone Gap, Virginia," said Larry, grinning.

Terry grinned back. Obviously, Big Stone Gap was just as strange a name as Medicine Hat.

"I'm a preacher's kid, too," said Larry, "and I'm just starting my junior year at Oral Roberts University down in Tulsa. Oral asked me to travel with him as his crusade organist for the summer, but my long-term goal is to travel overseas in missions ministry."

Wow, we've got a lot in common, Terry thought. They were both preachers' sons; both from small towns with corny names; both loved gospel music and saw some real possibilities for using it as a tool in overseas ministry.

But he's traveling with a big-time preacher and on his way to a degree, thought Terry. *I've only got three years of Bible school and a job on a ranch in the middle of nowhere. These guys are out of my league.*

"Have you ever considered going to ORU?" asked Larry. "We've got some materials out in the lobby. It's a really good school, better than you might think."

"I've heard it's a great place," replied Terry. "I'll pick up a brochure."

Don't kid yourself. That place costs a ton of money and you don't have any.

"I'll watch out for you," said Larry as the two shook hands again. Rehearsal break was over and he walked back up the steps to his seat at the organ.

* * *

It was seven o'clock when the music started, mingling with the noise of a full arena, and thirty minutes later a smiling Oral Roberts strode to the podium.

"God is a *good* God!" thundered Roberts. "I want you to know that, right from the start tonight. God is a *good* God!"

"Amen," the crowd responded loudly, and Terry felt himself stirring inside already. *One sentence and he's got everybody in the palm of his hand*, he thought. Then he remembered Kenneth Hagin's little books and wondered if all preachers down in Tulsa, Oklahoma, were so upbeat.

For the next 60 minutes, Roberts spoke of God's goodness, and of his desire to heal sick people, to heal the brokenhearted, and even to "heal" sinners of their sins. As soon as he had finished, hundreds of people began forming long lines so that Roberts could put his hands on their heads and pray for their healing.

Roberts was still praying for people at ten o'clock, when Terry remembered he had a six-hour drive back to the ranch. He was walking through the lobby, hoping that Ed would let him sleep-in just a little in the morning, when he saw a table piled with the brochures Larry had mentioned earlier that day.

No harm in taking one with me, Terry thought, picking up a brochure and unfolding it. Inside was a color photograph of the campus of Oral Roberts University, its center dominated by a gleaming blue, gold, and white tower that was topped by a flaming golden torch.

Wow, this is beautiful, thought Terry.

And then suddenly everything went into slow motion. Hundreds of people were filing past him out the doors, but he might as well have been alone for the stone silence that surrounded him. He heard nothing. Nothing but a single sentence that seemed to come not from without, but from somewhere inside him.

I want you to go to this school.

The power of these words shook Terry, as though he'd gotten hit by one of Ed's cattle prods.

This is your next step, said the voice. Again Terry shuddered, and this time he nearly dropped the brochure from his shaking hands.

God, I could never do this, he thought, clenching his eyes shut to steady himself. *ORU costs 1600 dollars a year, and I only make fifty bucks a week. I don't have that kind of money. It's impossible.*

You belong there. This is the direction you've prayed for.

* * *

As Terry collapsed into bed back at Ed's ranch just past four a.m., he remembered the first time God's voice had spoken to him.

God is going to use you. That's what Dwight McLaughlin had said back at the camp in Nanoose Bay, and the last ten years had proven that it really had been God speaking that night. Could it be happening again? Could God really be telling him that he was going to attend ORU? It just seemed too good to be true.

Well, you've been praying that you would hear God the way Ed hears him, haven't you?

He was drifting now, and it was hard to tell where thought stopped and dreams began. Then sleep came.

* * *

Summer was officially nearing an end, but the sun was still hot a month later when Ed and Terry were replacing some old fencing one morning out on the prairie. Terry had worked harder than ever before since that night in Edmonton. Not that he had embraced some new found work ethic. He was just so tense—so wound up day and night, by what he knew was God's impossible call to go to ORU. He had to work off all that energy somehow, and at this point in his life, there were no bombs to assemble or toilets to blow up. Instead, he felt like he himself might explode.

"Ed, I've got to talk to you about something serious. I don't know what to do," he said.

"Go ahead, son," Ed replied, sliding a post into a hole Terry had just dug. "You can tell me whatever you need to tell me."

Terry drove the auger into the clay deep enough for it to stick, and then stood back a foot.

"The Lord spoke to me last month, on the night I went to hear Oral Roberts in Edmonton. But I keep wondering how in the world...."

He took a deep breath.

"I believe God told me that I belong at Oral Roberts University."

Terry looked at Ed, but the man said nothing, and just kept looking at the ground for a long moment. When Ed looked back up, there were tears pooling in his eyes.

"Drop the auger and get in the truck," he said. "I have to show you something."

Ed started up the truck and pulled away. For the next two miles or so he kept silent, waiting until he had parked and pulled the emergency brake to speak again.

They were out in the middle of nowhere, and Terry wondered what could be happening. But he knew his boss well enough not to ask.

Sliding out of the truck, the two men walked about a hundred yards up an incline, when Ed stopped and pointed at something.

"You see that little hill over there?" asked Ed. "Two months ago, before you ever went to hear Oral Roberts, an angel appeared on that hill and told me you were supposed to go to ORU."

Ed's eyes moistened again, and he wiped them with his sleeve.

"I was surrounded by a light so bright it made me fall on my knees. And the angel said that I'm supposed to pay your way to Oral Roberts University for as long as you're there."

Terry was hit by a wave of emotion, and suddenly his eyes were as wet as Ed's. For a while the two men stood silent. Finally, Terry spoke.

"I can't believe it," he said quietly. "Kenneth Hagin was right. God knows I'm here and he *does* want to talk to me. And he even sent an actual *angel* ahead of time to tell you."

Ed smiled in an almost grandfatherly way.

"I didn't say anything because I wanted you to hear from the Lord for yourself," he said. "I couldn't do anything until that happened, and now it has."

* * *

Autumn became winter, and in mid-January 1968, Terry drove to Calgary and boarded a jet bound for Tulsa, Oklahoma. At last his time in the desert was over. He had finally heard God's voice, not from a burning bush, but from the lips of a humble cowboy with mud on his boots. He knew now that he was headed not only for Oral Roberts University, but into his destiny. He was sure of it.

This was the "something big" he had anticipated from the moment he had gotten home from Africa. What he did not know, as he waved a final goodbye to his folks and stepped on board the plane, was that he was leaving home in order to find it.

* * *

Terry had been at ORU for less than two months when something of an earthquake hit the religious world: On March 17, 1968, Oral Roberts left the Pentecostal Holiness denomination and announced his ordination by the United Methodist Church. Two days later, he fired the dean of ORU's School of Theology, and soon after that several other senior members of his crusade staff resigned their positions.

Stunned Pentecostal leaders around the world quickly denounced the move, and warned that in leaving his roots Oral Roberts might be embracing liberalism.

Questions flew. Did Roberts still believe in the divinity of Jesus and his virgin birth? Many liberal Methodists did not, and at least one of their bishops, James Pike, had recently been in the news for consulting a psychic to try and communicate with his dead son. Was Oral Roberts going to submit himself to that kind of authority?

Back home, Pentecostal Assemblies of Canada leaders reacted even more harshly, and some pastors warned their young people against attending ORU. Even the usually open-minded Bert and Ann Law were concerned. "Maybe you were wrong to enroll there," said his father when Terry called home. "Maybe you should get out of there and come home."

Had this been a big mistake? If church leaders withdrew their blessing from Oral Roberts, how would Terry ever find support for his own future mission work?

"Don't worry," Terry reassured his mother when she came to the phone. "Remember, God told Ed Stahl months ago that he was sending me here, long before any of this happened. And besides that I've just been invited to join Oral's crusade staff as their new song leader. Mum I'm the first student they've ever offered that position to. In fact I'm calling you from West Palm Beach, Florida! We're in the middle of a crusade here."

Terry had known his folks would be surprised—but he hadn't expected the silence coming from the other end of the line. There was a shuffling noise and a moment later he realized his dad had rejoined the call.

"Dad, I'm getting firsthand experience from one of the best evangelists in the world," he explained, "and besides that, I get to work hand-in-hand with Larry Dalton, that incredible musician I told you about last summer. This is such a great opportunity, and I know more than ever God brought me to ORU. I'm here to stay."

Another pause, and then muffled discussion in the background. Someone's hand was covering the receiver.

"All right, son," said Bert a moment or two later. "I think you might be right about this, but just be careful. A lot of folks up here are pretty upset with Oral Roberts."

Terry promised his father he would exercise caution, and said goodbye. He would have to wait until later to tell his folks the rest of the news: Instead of coming home to Canada for the summer, he would be accompanying Roberts to Europe and Israel as a member of the Collegians, ORU's student choir.

He *felt* confident. But what if associating with Roberts meant losing his good standing with the PAOC? Terry knew that was a possibility, but he had seen the big man behind the scenes often enough by now to know the rumors were wrong. Oral Roberts was as committed to Jesus as ever. And if in the future he ever had to choose between returning to the narrow-minded world of his childhood and exploring this bigger one, where following God could cost you something, he knew what he would do.

"Dad, put Mum on the phone, too," he asked, when he called his parents again a few weeks later to tell them about his upcoming trip.

"The Dean of Music has asked me to join the choir as their bass player," he explained, "and to preach in Oral's place in a couple of countries when he's elsewhere."

Then he dropped the even bigger bombshell on his folks. "We leave right after school lets out in May. We land in England, and go straight on to Denmark. But four days later we're taking a ferry from Finland to the Soviet Union, while Oral Roberts conducts some meetings in Kenya."

His parents gasped at the same time.

"Terry, the Russian government persecutes Christians," objected Bert. "That kind of trip could really be dangerous."

"I know Dad, but we're not going to Moscow," said Terry. "We'll be in the northwestern corner of the country—in a city called Tallinn in Estonia. It's the only place in the whole Soviet

Union where there are any Methodist churches, and Oral's connections got us in. Plus, we'll actually be safer without him being there."

Once again, Terry had managed to calm his parents' misgivings, even though he already had a secret sense that danger might indeed be a part of his upcoming journey.

In another few weeks, he would know for sure.

* * *

It was late on a rainy June night in the Soviet city of Tallinn when Terry and two of his friends slipped out of their run-down hotel to follow a new friend, Jon Karner, to a secret destination. Less than a week ago the group of forty students had landed in London, then sped across Denmark, Sweden, and Finland for four nights of concerts. Normally Terry would have found visiting new countries memorable, but they paled in comparison to the last few hours.

The group had arrived for their concert at the local Methodist church that evening, only to find it surrounded by armed soldiers. A new law had been passed, barring foreign visitors from speaking or singing in the church, the pastor had said, and would be in effect until they left the country. Nevertheless, he had insisted that the choir at least enter the building, if only to let the congregation see them for a few minutes.

Terry still found the scene inside the church hard to believe. Somehow at least 700 people of all ages had been crammed into a sanctuary built to seat 250. But it had been the teenagers and *babushkas*—little old ladies dressed in tattered sweaters and headscarves—that had grabbed his attention.

How could a church full of kids and grandmothers be a security threat? he had asked himself a half-dozen times, until one of the babushkas out in the congregation had started to sing. She sang in Estonian, of course, but it didn't matter. Everybody knew that melody, and at once, Terry and his fellow students had joined her in English.

On a hill far away stood an Old Rugged Cross
The emblem of suffering and shame...

For the first time in his life, Terry could see the "suffering and shame" of Christ's cross in that woman's wrinkled face. And that was when the answer to his question had hit him.

That's it! It's Jesus the communist government fears, not these people—it's the power of the Cross that's the real threat.

After that experience, accepting Jon's after-church invitation to an "underground" prayer meeting had been easy for Terry and two of his friends, Dale and Stan. For one thing, the group's hotel was crawling with KGB agents, government spies who made no attempt to conceal their purpose. The tall, lanky Estonian had risked his own safety just by showing up and waving them outside through the lobby window. Besides that, Terry had read somewhere that Christians behind the Iron Curtain risked their freedom by holding secret prayer meetings. The combination of Jon's bravery and his own appetite for adventure made the offer irresistible.

"We need to leave now," Jon whispered, hardly moving his lips. His coal-black hair and bushy beard reminded Terry of a disheveled Abe Lincoln.

"Follow me and do whatever I do," he said, and flipped up his collar as he stepped off the sidewalk into a cold drizzle that made the street glisten. Terry and the others followed a few paces back.

Two minutes later the four men were standing at a bus stop, when Terry noticed a fifth man standing twenty feet up the sidewalk, doing his best to be noticed.

"Don't look," whispered Jon, looking down at his shoes and pretending to shiver a little in the rain.

But it was hard not to look, considering that the spy up the sidewalk was wearing not only a trench coat and low-brimmed hat, but also sunglasses.

Sunglasses at ten o'clock at night, thought Terry. *He looks like Inspector Clouseau.* He turned away to stifle a grin, reminding himself that this was no game. The gun that was undoubtedly in this guy's pocket was as real as the soldiers' rifles he had seen three hours ago.

A long minute passed and finally a transit bus creaked to a stop and unfolded its rear door to let a man out and admit new fares.

"Not yet," whispered Jon, and Terry felt his pulse quicken and his leg muscles tighten.

The driver revved his engine and was starting to pull away when Jon moved.

"Now!" he huffed in a stage whisper as he jumped aboard, with Terry and the others clamoring behind him.

The door closed and they were off.

"Look behind us," said Jon, nodding his head sideways toward the bus' rear window.

Terry looked just in time to see the man in sunglasses sprinting down the street after them, waving his fist as he shrank into the night.

Thirty minutes later, after a bus transfer and a cramped, cloak-and-dagger car ride that purposely took ten miles to go three, their driver pulled his sardine can-sized compact car into an unlit parking lot.

"Wait here while I check around outside," ordered Jon, still whispering as he exited the front seat. His three charges stayed put in the back, and Terry squinted to see out the window. They were outside a tall, dilapidated looking apartment building that was identical to fifty others they had driven past in the last ten minutes.

After a moment the car door opened again.

"All clear," said Jon, "but we have to move quickly."

Seconds later Terry found himself hustling up flight after flight of dimly lit stairs, until the numbers on the apartment doors said ten-something.

How ironic that we have to climb ten stories to go "underground," he thought, as Jon tapped a signal on a door with his knuckles.

The door opened and everyone stepped inside. It was pitch black. Terry took two steps forward and tripped, almost falling. Instinctively, he realized it was someone's leg, although the person he had stepped on made no sound.

He stilled himself and listened, wondering how many people were present. He could hear lots of breathing, not only right beside him, but all over the room.

His eyes were adjusting now, and carefully he waded through a sea of blue jeans, dresses, and bare legs. At last he heard Jon whisper to sit, and he felt around until he found the seat of a wooden chair.

Everyone sat in silence for several minutes, until Jon told someone to turn on a floor lamp. But no sooner had the light come on than the sound of a truck engine rumbled up from the parking lot below, and everything went dark and still again.

"We can't take any chances," whispered Jon. "There are several people here who are not yet eighteen years old. That makes our meeting illegal."

Another five minutes passed and at last the lamp was turned back on. At least forty young people were standing or sitting, filling every available space, including the hallway and kitchen, in the little one-bedroom flat.

"Please tell us about America," someone asked. "Are there many young people in your churches? Our schools tell us that only old people go to church there."

No, that wasn't true, answered Terry. Millions of young people all over America went to church every Sunday, with no trouble from the authorities.

"What does it feel like to worship so freely?" asked a blonde-haired girl, who looked to be in her late teens.

"It's...it's hard to describe," replied Terry, looking over at Dale and Stan to see if they wanted to chime in. Neither opened his mouth, and Terry knew it was because of something Jon had told them in the car a few minutes earlier.

He had been more than halfway to his degree in architectural engineering when the KGB discovered that he had become his church's new youth leader. For that he had been expelled and his home raided several times by agents looking for Bibles.

Terry looked at Jon, who had been interpreting for him, and felt ashamed.

How do I tell them that we don't have any idea what our freedom means? he thought. *God help me. We're the ones who should be learning from them.*

Terry looked around the room at the young people eagerly awaiting his answer, and then thought of the youth group he had pastored back home in Medicine Hat.

Lord, you set that up, didn't you? All those months in the Hat weren't wasted at all—they were preparation for this. You were getting me ready to come to a place I would never have dreamed and will never forget.

"Worshiping the Lord with complete freedom is a privilege that no one can fully appreciate until it's threatened," he finally said. "And I wish our young people could come here to meet you as much as I wish I could take you home to meet them."

Maybe it hadn't been the glowing description they had hoped for, he thought. But at least it was the truth.

"Do you have any chewing gum wrappers?" asked one young man, and all around the room there were giggles at the puzzled look on Terry's face.

"We want to build a printing press," explained Jon. "We're saving the foil to make printing plates."

Jon knew his American guests were too dumbfounded to reply and announced in both English and Estonian that it was time to pray.

"I will interpret everyone's prayers as much as I can," he said.

One by one, the young people began to pray. The blonde-haired girl went first, praying in short sentences to give Jon time to keep up in English. But within two or three minutes she was pouring forth such emotion that she was forgetting to pause.

Jon looked at his guests and shrugged. "Don't worry about it," whispered Terry. "Just let them go."

For the next half hour the group took turns pouring their hearts out to God in their beautiful Estonian language. And even though he had no idea what they were saying, Terry found himself more moved by their prayers than any he had ever heard in his life.

At last it was time to leave, and while Jon checked the stair-well outside, Terry and his companions went around the apart-ment shaking hands, nodding and smiling at blessings they could not understand.

Finally, Jon came back and closed the door behind him.

"My driver friend will drop you off a few blocks from the hotel," he said. "It isn't safe for me to go back there tonight."

Terry looked up into the dark, haunting eyes of his new friend, who stood a full six inches taller than he.

"I can never thank you enough, Jon," he said. "Tonight has changed my life—our lives. And I hope we'll get to see each other again some day."

"Me too," said Jon, as he surprised Terry with a bear hug that almost lifted him off his feet. "Me too."

Then they were out the door and hurrying down ten flights of stairs.

God, if you ever call me back to this place, Terry prayed from the depths of his soul, *I vow to you I'll come.*

Jon's eyes had spoken volumes more than any of the magazine articles Terry had read about life behind the Iron Curtain. They were the eyes of someone older, full of suffering, yet still sparkling with joyful determination. But more than that, they had pierced him, and somehow linked the two men's souls.

Lord, I don't know if I have it in me to suffer the way Jon does, Terry thought. *But I want to know that strength, and that kind of joy. If suffering is the price...*

The sentence had not even fully formed itself before Terry knew the answer. He had seen something more than suffering in Jon's eyes—he had seen his own future, and yes, it would cost him. But somehow, it would be worth it.

CHAPTER 6

OUT OF AFRICA

IT WAS NEARING MIDNIGHT on New Year's Eve 1969, and Terry looked through his third-floor window at the coast of the Indian Ocean across the road. Moonlit whitecaps lapped peacefully at the shore. Only seven months after graduating with high honors from Oral Roberts University, he was back in Africa, where he and Dennis had ministered years earlier.

But it wasn't *South* Africa, the country he had been aiming for. Instead, he and Living Sound, his sixteen-member band, were stuck in a lonely little dot on the map called Beira, Mozambique, somewhere on Africa's eastern hip. And for the past ten nights this run-down motel, the Estoril, had been their unintended home.

Lord, how could everything go this wrong so fast? he prayed, as he broke bread for a special midnight communion with the team. *I don't understand. I've done my best to follow your lead. How could things get this messed up?*

Terry poured the wine into the goblet he had borrowed from the restaurant downstairs. He had asked for grape juice, but apparently no one at the Estoril knew a word of English and he sure didn't speak their tribal dialect.

He looked across the room at Jan, his wife of eleven months, as she sat with Larry and the others. Their heads were bowed and their eyes closed, and Terry knew they were all asking God the same thing: *Why us?*

The past year had been a dream come true—until this nightmare.

Terry and Jan had been married in January, two days before the start of ORU's spring semester. Three weeks later, he and Larry Dalton had assembled the student musical ensemble that had become Living Sound, his dream team for overseas missions. The team's summer tour following graduation had been a rousing success, and over those four and a half months they had saved the $18,000 needed to come to Africa. Best of all, though, had been when Terry had said goodbye to his dad.

"I'm proud of you son," Bert had said, pulling Terry into the first fatherly hug he was able to remember. "I love you."

The moment had emblazoned itself in Terry's heart like some glowing, golden seal of approval...which only made his present situation worse.

Why do these guys have to suffer from my mistakes? he wondered as he looked around the room. Bo, Bev, newlyweds Dale and Honeybee—more than half of Living Sound's 16 members had dropped out of ORU at the school year's end to be part of Terry's and Larry's new venture. Some had sacrificed full scholarships.

I've let every one of them down—especially Jan.

It had been Terry's plan to go to nearby Rhodesia, after the way into South Africa had been blocked. At the time, he'd thought, *No problem. I can still make this happen...*

Terry grimaced as he thought about his in-laws back in Florida. Like everyone else back home, they assumed their daughter and her new husband were traveling around southern Africa, giving concerts and witnessing to their faith in Jesus.

Albert would never have let me marry her, if he knew I'd get her into this kind of mess, he lamented. *And even if I could place a call, how would I explain?*

Terry looked at Jan again and remembered the moment they had met a year and a half earlier. He had been standing at the rail of the ferry, watching Tallinn's harbor recede in the distance as ORU's choir left the Soviet Union, and had decided to tell whoever was standing next to him about the silent vow he had made at Jon's secret prayer meeting two nights earlier. It was Jan.

"If God ever calls me to come back here I will," he'd said. "No matter what it takes I'll come."

"I believe you," Jan had replied. That was all she'd said, but there was something about her smile, so gentle and full of mercy, that had captivated him. After that he had pursued every chance to be with her.

He thought back to their first touch in downtown London and their first kiss in that garden in Old Jerusalem.

Lord, I don't know who tied the donkey to that tree, he'd thought, *but I know you arranged it.*

Neither of them had seen the animal when they walked past it, and its sudden braying had startled Jan so badly she had jumped into Terry's arms. He'd kissed her and the rest had been history.

It was five minutes to midnight now, and Terry asked his baritone, Roy, to lead the group in a song while he served the communion bread and the wine.

Oh, the blood of Jesus
Oh, the blood of Jesus
Oh, the blood of Jesus
It washes white as snow.

Roy could be singing on national television with Oral Roberts right now, thought Terry. But it wasn't only Roy. These young people were among ORU's best students, and they had left everything behind to follow him, only to wind up marooned halfway around the world in Mozambique.

God, the way we started—the prophecy in Kansas City—we all thought it was you speaking.

* * *

That first weekend back in February had been a life-changer for everyone.

Terry's nameless collection of students had only learned five songs, and were two hours late for their opening concert on Friday evening at Pastor Powell's little church. Yet by Sunday night, God had used them to bring sixty people to Jesus, had given them their name and called them "kings."

During that Sunday morning concert, just as the team had finished singing and he was stepping up to preach, a man's voice had boomed from the back of the church, prophetically.

"I have ordained you to go to the nations. There will come a time when you are homeless, but don't be afraid. I have called you to the nations as kings to conquer."

* * *

Lord, we can't get anymore homeless than being stuck in Beira, thought Terry. The past ten days had held the strangest turn of events in his life.

For months, the South African government had refused to grant the group's visas. In their minds, American university students were anti-war hippies, and they didn't want rabble-rousers in their country.

But in no time, Terry had come up with another plan: Living Sound could start out in neighboring Rhodesia, since visas weren't required there. He'd felt proud of his ingenuity.

"We'll do a series of concerts in their capital, and prove our good will," Terry had told the team. "Within a few weeks we ought to be able to drive on down to South Africa."

But who could have foreseen Rhodesia's diplomatic struggle with Washington, especially while Living Sound was *en route*? The airport immigration authorities at Salisbury International had retaliated by refusing them entry and shuttling them back on board the plane—next stop, Beira, Mozambique.

* * *

Terry looked at his watch. 11:58 p.m. Time to pray out the Sixties and pray in the Seventies. He had often wondered how the team might begin the new decade, but he could never have dreamed of—*this*.

Everyone ate the bread and drank the wine, and then Terry led a prayer.

"God, we don't understand what's going on," he began, as the bell at a nearby mission began to count twelve. "But that prophecy back in Kansas City said there would come a time when we would be homeless. Well, here we are, and now we're counting on you to bring the rest of it to pass. If you've called us as kings to conquer, you're going to have to make it happen. Because we can't."

And so 1970 arrived as the twelfth bell sounded and the group sat silent, listening for sounds from outside.

"Honey, did you hear that?" whispered Jan. "Is that fireworks going off?"

Terry walked to the window and looked out along the coastline towards town.

"It's too muffled, kind of like a thump. And there are no flashes in the sky," he said.

And then Terry recognized the thumps for what they were—the beating of tribal drums. They were coming from the little cluster of mud huts behind the Estoril, where most of the motel staff lived. If he felt far from home five minutes ago, these sounds from another age flung him further still. Living Sound was already out of place, but now they had been thrown out of time, as well.

"Lord, where are you in all of this?" Terry muttered under his breath. "Have you forgotten us?"

* * *

The sky was a brilliant blue on the morning of January 5th, as Terry finished his breakfast and left the Estoril to hail a taxi to Beira's airport immigration office. Would he run face first into the same stone wall he'd met for the past three weeks?

Jan and the rest of the team headed across the road to the beach.

At least the ocean is free, Terry thought. Living Sound's tab at the Estoril had just topped $2,000, and he had no idea how he was going to pay it, much less get the group to Rhodesia or South Africa—or even back to the States—anywhere but here in Mozambique. To make things worse, their musical gear and all their luggage other than carry-ons were still in diplomatic limbo. They couldn't go anywhere until Terry persuaded the local officials to cooperate.

This whole process is so ridiculous, he thought, as he gazed out the window of the beat-up cab and rehearsed what had become his morning ritual.

I'll be standing at the door when they open. Then I'll wait outside the customs office until the little man decides to come out. But he won't even acknowledge my presence until he climbs onto his throne.

A desk wasn't enough—he actually had a throne. If the situation hadn't been so dire, Terry would have enjoyed watching the obese little official wheezing his way up to his carved wooden perch. The man liked making a show of his authority over foreigners—especially a whole group of Americans.

He'll take my papers and look at them like he's never seen them before, thought Terry. *And then he'll hand them back and say, "No." And that will be it.*

Terry paid the cabbie and waited outside the immigration office, Right on cue, the official appeared. But this time he didn't bother ascending his throne.

"You and your group are being deported back to the United States," said the man in heavily accented English.

"Sir, wait..." Terry started to object.

But the official continued. "The Rhodesian government says it warned Trans World Airlines that you were not welcome before you ever left America, and therefore the airline must bear the cost of your stay here, and also return you to your country."

And that was that.

* * *

It was snowing two nights later, when Terry and his exhausted team landed at Kennedy Airport in New York and walked out of the arrivals terminal to the curb. According to headlines he had glimpsed in an airport newspaper box, the city was experiencing record cold temperatures.

Terry looked over at Jan, shivering in her short-sleeved sun dress. Her olive complexion had turned a dark copper under the

African sun, and now there were goose bumps dotting her arms.

Some husband you are, he thought. In anger, he kicked a clump of snow.

"God this isn't fair," he muttered. *We spent nearly five months raising all that money to get to Africa, without any help from Oral Roberts, and now it's gone. And all our luggage and equipment are on the other side of the world. We don't even have enough money left to get back to Tulsa. It's not fair.*

If it hadn't been for an influential board member Terry had called from the airport, not even the Teen Challenge drug rehab center 90 miles south in Philadelphia would have agreed to take the group in.

When the airport limo pulled up, Terry handed the driver a wad of small bills and change he had collected from the rest of the team.

Ninety minutes later they were all standing in the hallway of Teen Challenge's old brownstone in downtown Philadelphia, waiting for someone to assign them rooms. Terry had no idea how many nights he could keep the team here.

He extended his hand to the center's director as he came down the stairs to receive the team, but no handshake followed.

"I don't want you around my young men," the man snapped.

Terry stepped back in dismay.

"Look at your men's long hair and these women's skimpy dresses. You're exactly the wrong influence for these boys who are trying to get their lives straightened out. If I didn't have to do it I wouldn't let you stay here for a single night. So just go to your rooms and stay away from our people."

Terry looked at the man and started to reply, but he was just too tired to speak.

The director handed out several room keys, and then spoke again.

"Breakfast is at seven-thirty. Be on time and sit by yourselves. Now, follow me upstairs, and keep quiet."

Terry looked at Jan and his jet-lagged team. It was clear that nothing mattered to any of them other than getting some sleep.

"Just do as he says," said Terry in a whisper.

He felt defeated.

* * *

"This is even worse than Beira," one of the guys complained the following Friday evening, as the group gathered for prayer. Everyone nodded in agreement. At least in Mozambique they had been able to get some sun and make a few friends among the locals. But here? The director obviously ruled with an iron fist, and his whole staff had been just about as hateful. Worst of all, Terry still hadn't been able to find alternative accommodations.

"My folks want me to come home," someone else said. "They say we ought to just admit we were wrong and disband the group."

"Mine, too," said one of the girls. "I mean, we can't just start touring again and ask all those churches for more money. We don't even have our instruments."

"Let's wait a little longer," said Terry. "If something doesn't give soon, I'll find a way to get everyone home. In the meantime, tomorrow is Saturday, so let's all just skip the ugly stares at breakfast and sleep in."

Terry was fast asleep the next morning, when a loud banging on his door woke him.

"Who is it?" he asked, wondering what had gone wrong now.

"It's five till eight," yelled the director, rattling the doorknob from the hallway outside. "Why aren't you people downstairs in the chapel?"

Quietly, Terry cracked open the door.

"You told us to stay away from your young men," replied Terry. "We're just following orders."

"That's no excuse," growled the director. "Chapel service starts at 8 a.m. Tell everyone to get dressed and be downstairs in five minutes."

If Terry had felt defeated before, he felt crushed now.

All you can do is let yourself and your team be ordered around, he thought, as he trudged down the stairs. Everything was falling apart right in front of his eyes.

Might as well face the truth. It's over.

A young man with a guitar was leading a song when Terry and the team trudged into the back of the oversized living room that served as Teen Challenge's chapel.

"Just sit in the last couples of rows," Terry whispered as his beleaguered teammates filed past him through the door.

Two songs later, the young man up front put down his guitar and then stepped back to the microphone.

"We've got a surprise guest speaker with us this morning," he announced. "This is Pastor Rodney Whittle, from Minneapolis. He called me from the airport last night and said that God told him and his wife to come to Philadelphia, and that mine was the only local phone number they had. He asked me if there was some place he could minister, and I told him about this morning's service—so here he is."

A fiftyish-looking gentleman in a gray suit and tie stepped to the microphone and began to speak.

"I don't exactly know why I'm here this morning," said Pastor

Whittle in a gentle voice. "All I know is that God spoke to my wife and me night before last and told us to come to Philadelphia. So I guess I'll just start by telling you my story."

He had once presided over a successful congregation belonging to a conservative denomination, Whittle said. "But I had grown cold, and my ministry had become nothing more than my profession. Then one Saturday as I sat in my office I realized that if I wasn't scheduled to preach the next day I probably wouldn't even go to church.

"It was a moment of reckoning, and I asked God what I could do to get back to my true calling. What happened next was hard to believe, but I knew I'd better obey.

"God told me to resign my church and move to Minneapolis, so I did. My wife and three daughters and I moved into a cold-water apartment, because it was all we could afford, now that I didn't have a job. A few days later I started selling vacuum cleaners door to door."

Terry looked over at his teammates. They all seemed as depressed as he was.

I should've just let them sleep, he thought.

"What do you do when you know God has called you, yet it appears as though he is taking away that calling?" asked Whittle. "What do you do when you pray, but there's only silence in return?"

This jerked Terry to attention. *Are you kidding me?* he thought. These were the very questions he'd asked over and over for the past month.

He couldn't know a thing about us, thought Terry, *and if the director told him something about us it wouldn't be anything good. For all he knows, we're seeking drug treatment like everyone else in the room. Lord, what's happening here?*

Terry looked over at Jan, who had begun weeping, and realized there were tears on the faces of other team members, as well. Even Larry's eyes were brimming—something Terry had never seen—and the sight caused a lump in his own throat.

For the next half-hour, Pastor Whittle explained how God had used his job as a door-to-door salesman to restore his love for hurting people. Eventually he had established a vibrant new church in Minneapolis, where his ministry was far more effective than he had ever dreamed it could be.

"God is faithful," said Whittle, as though he knew everything Terry and the team had been going through. "Even when he is completely silent, he is still there with you. And when it seems like he's broken all his promises and revoked his calling, he will remain faithful to make that calling a reality. But sometimes we've got to come to the end of *our* plans, in order for God to accomplish *his* plan."

Terry was as choked up as the others when the service dismissed, and as soon as he could, he corralled Pastor Whittle and the team into a nearby reading room full of old sofas.

"Sir, you've just told our whole story," said Terry, his voice breaking with emotion. "We've just spent the last month wondering why God would call us to Africa, and take us all the way there just to send us home broke with no way to get back."

"Tell me everything," said Pastor Whittle.

Terry sped through the past eleven months in ten minutes, from the highs of Living Sound's first weekend in Kansas City to the humiliation of their deportation from Mozambique and current exile in Philadelphia. By the time he finished, Whittle was shedding tears of his own.

"What is it that you really want from God?" the pastor asked.

"What's your *true* calling?"

"All we ever really wanted was to go to South Africa," interjected Larry, and all around him heads nodded in agreement.

"He's right," said Terry. "We were only going to Rhodesia as a bridge to get to South Africa. But that's where we really felt called to go."

Pastor Whittle closed his eyes and sat quietly for a long moment. It was obvious something was brewing inside him. Then he looked up and pointed his finger across the coffee table directly at Terry.

"In one week, you're going to be in Johannesburg, South Africa," he said, in a tone more firm and authoritative than he had used all morning.

Terry was stunned, and for a second he felt like he was back in Kansas City, when that first prophecy had been spoken.

"Sir, we all want to believe you," said Terry. "But the South African government has repeatedly refused to grant our visas, and we don't have the money to buy airplane tickets even if they did."

"You heard me," said Whittle, who was smiling now, as though a big load had been lifted off his shoulders.

"In one week, you're going to be in Johannesburg. I know now why the Lord spoke to me to come here. And I know that what I'm telling you is going to happen."

Terry stood to his feet, with the rest of the team quickly following his cue.

"We know you've got a plane to catch, Pastor," he said, as he walked the reverend to the door. "We don't want to hold you and your wife up any longer."

Whittle said thanks, and shook everyone's hand, before disappearing down the stairs that led to the Teen Challenge office. As soon as he was gone, Terry turned to see that the whole team had sat back down. It was obvious they all needed a chance to respond.

"This entire morning feels like a dream," said Larry. "How in the world are we going to get to Johannesburg in a week?"

"Look, if God could speak through that man so specifically in describing our situation, then we might as well believe he can get us there," responded Jim, who, at eighteen, was the youngest member of the team.

"Jim's right," said Terry. "The Bible says, 'faithful is he who calls you, who also will bring it to pass.' If what Pastor Whittle said is really from the Lord, then somehow he's going to do it. We've just got to wait and see."

"Honey, do you really think what that pastor said is going to happen?" whispered Jan that evening, as she kissed Terry goodnight.

"I'm finished with trying to figure anything out," said Terry. "Let's just sleep on it, and then take things one day at a time."

But did he dare to let the vision be re-ignited? The wellbeing of the whole group rested heavily on his shoulders.

* * *

It was nearing dinnertime three days later, when Terry hustled the team into his and Jan's bedroom. He hadn't felt this kind of excitement since five minutes before landing in Rhodesia, just before they'd been abruptly turned away.

"You guys are not going to believe what just happened!" he nearly shouted. "This morning I got called down to the office for a phone call from the U.S. State Department. I don't know how they found us, but they said they've been searching for us to tell us that a few days ago South Africa suddenly decided to grant our visas! I had no idea they were even reconsidering it, but somehow they took another look at our applications and decided to say *yes*."

"When did they do it?" asked one of the team. "If it was last week, then they granted our visas *before* Pastor Whittle ever came here."

"It doesn't matter, because we still don't have plane tickets," said bass singer Bo Melin, who had seemed even more discouraged than the others. "I hope I'm being realistic, and not just a doubting Thomas. But I'll believe it when we're standing in the airport in Johannesburg."

"Yes, but wait—I got *two* phone calls," said Terry, feeling like he might burst at any moment. "That's why I said you're not going to believe it.

"A pastor friend of mine out in California heard about what we've been going through, and without telling anybody he just decided to call SwissAir. He said he felt led to do it. Anyway, SwissAir has offered to issue us round-trip tickets to South Africa on credit, and they say we can pay them back when we have the money!"

"Oh, come on!" said Ron, who was wide-eyed and starting to laugh. "Airlines don't give credit to strangers—especially a group of broke college kids."

"Yeah, well. They just did!" said Terry. "Whittle was right. And we are already booked on a flight to Johannesburg this Saturday. It will be exactly one week after he told us we would go!"

By the next April, Terry was feeling like he had just spent three months in heaven on earth. The team had landed in Johannesburg on Monday, January 16, 1970, and hit the ground running with three days of outdoor concerts, before accepting an invitation to minister at a drug-riddled high school for a whole week after that.

"Jesus is the real 'high' you've been looking for," Terry had preached to the 900 students at Klerksdorp's Milner High, and more than 600 of them had made public commitments to Christ over the five days Living Sound had been with them.

That amazing response, and the instant halt in drug trafficking amongst the students, had landed the team in the Johannesburg newspapers. Suddenly invitations to perform were coming from as far south as Cape Town.

"I feel like Jesus' disciples must have felt when they caught so many fish their boat started to sink," Terry told a Johannesburg housewife named Joy Heaton, who volunteered to manage the correspondence Bible courses the team had begun handing out.

"Well you should," said Joy, "because you've even received more than 300 responses from a town you've never been to. Evidently, a young girl who gave her life to God at your concert in one town moved to another and started telling her friends at school all about the Lord. That makes about three thousand new followers of Jesus in your first three months!"

"Well, we're on our way to Springs now," said Terry. "The pastor there says his church is going to be packed out, so let's see how many more fish we can catch this time."

Springs Full Gospel Church was built to seat 400 people, but there were at least 650 filling every available space in the auditorium when Living Sound began their 45-minute set the next Sunday evening. As was his custom, Terry stayed behind in the prayer room to gather his thoughts before going onstage to preach.

"God, you've been so gracious," he prayed as he knelt down and spread his notes out on the floor to give them a final once-over. Beyond the wall in front of him, he could hear Jim singing Audrey Meier's song, "To be Used of God," the solo he had sung that first weekend in Kansas City, more than a year before. Somehow the song triggered a sense of history in him, and for a moment he forgot about his notes and closed his eyes to think back over his life and pray.

"Lord, how could I ever have expected that you would use a no-name rebel like me to bring thousands of young people to yourself? Or that you'd speak to Dwight McLaughlin, who didn't even know me, or send an angel to Ed Stahl, or let me work with Oral Roberts? God, I could never have imagined any of it, but you knew.

"And look where you've brought us. Here we are in South Africa! It took three trips across the ocean, but you did it. You brought us here, and right outside that wall there's yet another auditorium packed with people for me to call to Christ."

I'm going to send you behind the Iron Curtain, and you will do things most people will consider impossible, said a voice, interrupting his reverie.

"Oh God!" Terry gasped, and then slowly began to lean forward, as though a yoke had been placed on his shoulders. Within moments he had buried his face in his Bible. There was no point in looking up to see who was speaking—the voice hadn't come from outside, but within. He felt as if every cell in his body could hear.

There was also no point in asking how such an impossible thing would be accomplished, because he already knew the answer. He knew because of Philadelphia, and Beira, and Kansas City—because of Jon, and McLaughlin, and Ed, and Pastor Whittle. God had already brought him through so many storms in his life, and now he had a team who had followed him into the biggest one of all, only to emerge stronger, bolder, and full of vision for their future.

The question was—would they embrace a vision as ridiculous as taking a high-volume concert ensemble into communist lands where Christians had to meet in secret just to whisper their prayers? Could *he* even comprehend it?

The music stopped and it was time to preach.

In five minutes I'll know, thought Terry, trembling, as he walked out of the prayer room and stepped onto the podium. Everyone would know. Because there was no way he could utter a single word of the sermon he had worked so long to prepare until he let this—this *news bulletin* out from behind his ribcage.

I'm going to send you behind the Iron Curtain, and you will do things most people will consider impossible.

"Father, help me," Terry whispered as he approached the microphone and looked down at Jan and the team, who had taken their seats on the front row.

Lord, we've always voted on everything till now, thought Terry, as he realized the milestone he was about to mark in proclaiming this drastic change in Living Sound's direction. Given a vote, he knew the team would say no, just as Israel would have voted to return to Egypt when they saw the Red Sea, and David's brothers would have talked him out of challenging Goliath. No, there was no avoiding it. He had to declare it.

There comes a time for daredevils instead of diplomats, a time when the very saying of a thing brings the grace that makes it happen. Terry knew that tonight was such a time.

Indeed, the next few minutes would bring the seeding of a vision that grace alone could bring to flower. One that would take Terry and future teams not only inside the Iron Curtain, but eventually put him before the cameras on Moscow's evening news. More important still, tonight's divine encounter would serve to sharpen the hearing of a man who, in years to come, would need to listen keenly to the one voice that could both convey him to the heights and console him in the depths.

For although he could not know it at that moment, Terry's future held the extremes of both.

CHAPTER 7

CRACK IN THE CURTAIN

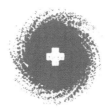

JUST AS TERRY HOPED, the shock of his startling declaration that Living Sound would minister behind the Iron Curtain ignited excitement within the team. Returning home from South Africa at the end of 1970 for Christmas with their families, they were already eager to witness God's hand in the next chapter of their ministry. Considering how the Lord had brought them through Mozambique and Philadelphia to the past ten months of amazing success in South Africa, what did he have in store for them now?

Terry was excited, too, and as soon as he had rented a Tulsa apartment, he made an appointment to see Oral Roberts. The big man would be proud of his former protégé, he assured himself, as he kissed Jan goodbye and stepped out into the frosty cold of an early December morning.

Sitting outside Roberts' office, Terry rehearsed the statistics to himself several times during the ten-minute drive to ORU. He had to get them right, not to brag, but to bless Oral, especially considering their last visit fourteen months earlier.

We gave 350 concerts, handed out ten thousand Bible correspondence courses, and there probably were thousands more converts who didn't register....

Would Roberts be pleased, or would Terry meet with the same barbed reaction that he'd gotten once before? He tried not to feel anxious.

Fifteen months earlier, Terry had left a concert tour in Arkansas to travel back to Tulsa for a Friday morning appointment with Oral in his big office overlooking the campus. The trip had meant getting Ron, his drummer, to drive all night so he could get some sleep, but the hope that Roberts might underwrite the group's upcoming mission to Africa had made it seem worthwhile. If everything went right, they would both be back in Little Rock by suppertime on Saturday.

Yes, it had been a good plan. Except for hitting that dead horse in the middle of the road at one a.m., totaling a borrowed car, and spending half the night in the hospital. But he had made the appointment right on time, at 9 a.m.

"He will see you now," smiled Oral's long-time secretary, Ruth Rooks.

Hobbling into Roberts' office, bandaged up and on crutches, Terry had felt beat up but excited to share his vision for South Africa. Oral would see what a true "road warrior for God" looked like.

Or so he'd hoped.

"I feel sorry for you, Terry, but this is just a consequence of getting ahead of God," Oral had begun, before launching into a twenty-minute lecture on presumption and poor planning. It might have gone on even longer if he hadn't turned and seen the look on his bruised and bandaged former student's face.

"You're going to South Africa, aren't you?" Oral had said in a suddenly softer tone. "I can see it."

"Yes sir, I am," replied Terry.

"You've got a powerful calling on your life," Oral had said. Then he had walked over and laid his hands on Terry's head, and prayed for healing in his body, and God's blessing and miraculous intervention in bringing his vision to fruition.

Terry had left Oral's office without a penny that morning, but he'd gained the man's respect, which had proven far more valuable since then.

* * *

Now, as he pushed the button on the private elevator that would take him to the top floor of ORU's tallest building, he thought, *Oral's going to be so excited.*

But some things—like Oral Roberts' penchant for coming to the point—never changed.

"Terry, this is all good and I'm happy for you," Roberts interjected about three minutes into his former student's speech, before dropping the bomb.

"What are you going to do next?"

It was just seven words with a question mark, but it blew the ground from beneath Terry's feet.

"I...uh...Larry and I are planning to take the team to Europe next...."

"Terry, let me tell you what I've seen," Roberts interrupted.

"I've watch dozens, maybe hundreds, of ministries meet with rousing success at first, and then decide to just keep repeating it over and over. And it works well enough, so they get comfortable and lazy. But eventually their *faith* stops growing, and their ministry follows suit. And after a while they just fade away."

Terry knew it was true, because he'd seen it happen. And he had also watched Oral do exactly the opposite, abandoning his tent crusades and church music in favor of prime-time TV specials with choreographed pop singers. But what he didn't know was that Oral was about to touch a branding iron to his future.

"Terry, there's one thing that makes faith grow," said Oral, leaning forward in his chair, "and that's walking straight into whatever it is that everyone else is running from. And I'll tell you what I've learned and what I've lived by: You've got to make plans that are so big that when you go to sleep at night, they'll scare you to death if God isn't in them."

* * *

Roberts' words had emblazoned themselves across Terry's mind like a stamp on his forehead, when the time came for Living Sound to resume traveling the next June. But they were also weighing him down.

Oral gave a perfect description of my call to take Living Sound behind the Iron Curtain, he told himself as he lay awake one night.

Mozambique was an afternoon shower compared to the potential storm of problems that loomed ahead. At least back in Beira he had known where to go and what questions to ask. But finding a way to take a full-stage ensemble into some police state where people were afraid to pray out loud? Where do you go to learn that? He felt like a blind man in a lifeboat during a hurricane. But wasn't that pretty much the same predicament Jesus' disciples were in when he calmed the storm?

Lord, you were actually in the boat with them, he thought, *so they shouldn't have been afraid.*

That was Oral's real point wasn't it? He had just stated it in the reverse—panicking if God's *wasn't* in his plan actually meant being fearless if he *was* in it.

Lord, I know you're in this plan, because it was yours from the start, he prayed. *You were the one who spoke to me back in South Africa, so it doesn't matter how big the storm gets. You're in charge. It's your boat and your storm, and if it takes facing a bigger storm to grow in your grace, then that's what I'm willing to do.*

And then he slept well.

* * *

With fear now out of the equation, Terry had a spring in his step on the morning that Living Sound loaded up their "new" used Greyhound bus and headed down the highway. The old coach was a huge, split-level beast, but the newly expanded team needed it. Thanks to Larry's adding a brass section, they had grown in number from 16 to 23, and with the August arrival of tiny Misty Rochelle Law, they were 24.

Terry felt excited to be on the road again, and he filled his preaching with stories about the miracle of Mozambique and God's blessing in South Africa. Everywhere Living Sound went, they seemed to gain new found respect and support. Yet Terry's increased responsibilities as a leader, husband, and now father, still occasionally weighed him down, especially given his challenging call to Communist lands.

If God has really called us to go behind the Iron Curtain, he reminded himself frequently, *then he has to open the way. I'm not going to try and force it.*

But then he would waffle, and start dreaming up another scheme.

"Honey, sometimes I wonder if I ought to take some kind of concrete action to get our visas for Russia," he confided in Jan one evening, as she nursed Misty. "Or maybe I should call Professor

Durasoff at ORU. He's been over there a bunch of times."

"Yes, but he's also been kicked out a bunch of times," Jan reminded him.

It was true. Steve Durasoff had told Terry how he'd been banned from the Soviet Union "for life" several times, but always managed to sneak back in at a different border crossing than he had used before.

"I guess we can't sneak a whole team and all our instruments in," Terry mused, "and I have no idea of what kind of danger I'd be putting us in. I don't know—it just seems more impossible than ever."

"You've said over and over that God will take care of it," said Jan. "So just stay committed and it'll work out."

"You're right," replied Terry, taking a long look at his wife as she cradled Misty in her bosom. When they'd first met he had been bowled over by Jan's dark eyes and sultry voice. But this was her true beauty. Somehow she always found a way to calm the mischievous kid from Parkside that was still a part of him—the one that wanted to run outside and catch a lightning bolt in his hand every time there was a storm.

"You know, I grew up thinking you were saved by grace, but after that you were pretty much on your own," he said, and Jan chuckled. "It's hard just waiting, and depending on God to come through without my help."

Terry gave an embarrassed little snort of his own. Admitting his pride just made it sound as stupid as it really was.

* * *

In June 1972, the team was in southern California, setting up their gear for an evening concert, when Terry announced that their bimonthly batch of mail had arrived from the office back in Tulsa. He enjoyed passing out everyone's letters from home. Considering that they were all sacrificing so much to fulfill their mission, it felt good to play Santa once in awhile.

"Here's one for you, Barbi," he said as he thumbed through the stack of letters. "Tim. Bev. Ronnie, here's one from Canada. Another one for Bev, and two for Larry. And...hey, what's this? This one's from somewhere overseas."

Terry studied the red ink stamped on the white business envelope in his hands. He and Larry had already set up a fall tour that would take the team across western Europe, and he had learned to recognize the post marks from Sweden, Germany, and the rest. This was a different alphabet than he'd ever seen, though, with slashes and accents attached to otherwise familiar letters.

"I think it's from Poland!" he said—and at once the others stopped reading and formed in a circle around him.

Terry studied the letter, hoping to spot words that looked at least a little familiar.

"It's definitely from Poland," he said. "Krakow, Poland. Let's see...*uniwersytet Jagiellonski, klub, 3*...something 1972. You guys—there's a school called Jagiellonian University in Poland. I've heard of it before. And I think we just got invited to sing in some kind of club there on the third of whatever *listopada* means. Holy cow, we're going behind the Iron Curtain!"

God was clearly opening a new door, thanks to Terry's obedience in heeding Oral Roberts' counsel. How could he ever have dreamed that this great man would become as much of a mentor to him as his own dad? Then again, Bert and Oral were both true pioneers, thought Terry. They just blazed trails through different fields.

Maybe I'm a pioneer too. Maybe God has called me to cut some new path where nobody has ever thought to go.

* * *

It was foggy and cold in Old Krakow on the first Friday night of November, and the dampness of the concrete basement where Terry was being interrogated made it even colder.

"You are spies! You are from the CIA!" yelled the director of the *Klub Pod Jaszczurami*, as he paced back and forth in front of the little table where Terry sat.

Lord, this is like a bad spy movie, thought Terry, as he sat riveted in the room's only chair and surveyed his surroundings. Dangling from the flaking plaster ceiling above him, a bare light bulb seemed to rob the already drab room of all color.

"No, sir, we're not spies," insisted Terry calmly for the tenth time in half an hour. "We're musicians, and we're just here to perform two concerts. You invited us."

"No, you *are* spies!" the director hissed in crisp, sibilant English. "Why do you people come here with your message when you know we are not allowed to accept it? Why are you confusing the audience?"

"You knew we were a Christian group when you invited us," countered Terry, resisting the urge to grin at his angry host's predicament. Of course, they hadn't known Living Sound was Christian, anymore than Terry had known that the club was owned and operated by the Polish Youth Communist Party.

"The Party does not invite religious groups," growled the director, raising his voice to counter the volume of the song Living Sound was performing upstairs. "We thought you were an American rock and roll group!"

"Well, listen to them," replied Terry, pointing upward. "That's a rock song they're singing right now."

He looked at his watch. It was 6:15 p.m. and the team had launched into the final song of their sold-out first concert. In another forty-five minutes, they were supposed to begin again.

God is moving by his Spirit
Moving through all the earth
Signs and wonders when God moveth
Move O Lord in me...

"That sounds like rock music to me," yelled Terry as the song built to a crescendo. Even with the closed door at the top of the stairs, the sound had gotten loud enough to momentarily stop the argument.

Lord, this is amazing, thought Terry. He knew what was coming next.

God...(trumpets and trombones blasted a punctuating fill)
Is moving!...(a longer fill)
By...(the eight singers sounded like eighty)
His Spirit!...(an electric guitar wailed above the trumpets)
Moving...through all the earth!

The song finished, and the old gothic hall upstairs fell quiet for several seconds before the club's director started to resume his diatribe.

"This is not allowed...."

The cheering above erupted like a thunderclap. Except that it kept rumbling when it should have died down...and then gradually resolved into the rhythmic, unison clapping that in Europe signifies the demand for an encore.

Go for it, guys! Terry grinned, wondering if he could suppress the urge to laugh out loud. Sure enough, he heard Ron give his snare drum a hard *whack whack*, signaling a reprise of the group's final song.

Terry looked at the director and his two sidekicks, who had turned their attention from him and were staring at the ceiling, as if they were wondering when their agony would ever end.

> *Signs and wonders when God moveth*
> *Move O Lord in me*
> *Hallelujah, Hallelujah*
> *Amen!*

The encore was over, but this time the ensuing roar was instantaneous, and continued for so long that Terry might have felt a little embarrassed, had he not been overwhelmed with sheer awe. Nowhere in England or Europe, or even in the stadiums in South Africa, had Living Sound's music ever evoked this kind of response. Then again, he was sure no public proclamation of the gospel had ever taken place here in Poland like the one he had launched into near the beginning of the concert.

Terry had been scheduled to speak for about ten minutes after Living Sound opened with a medley of Dionne Warwick's "What the World Needs Now" and a couple of other current American pop hits. He would follow with some prepared notes on Chopin and Copernicus and other famous Poles the world admired, and then end his talk with a brief mention of the group's faith in God. But the songs had fallen flat and he had run through his notes in less than two minutes. Standing there in front of a packed house full of college students—many of whom seemed to understand English pretty well—Terry had remembered the vow he had made years earlier that there would never be another Murray Ingham, someone he waited too late to tell about Christ. And knowing that this might be these young Polish students' only chance to hear the gospel, he had deliberately shocked everyone from the audience to the team standing onstage behind him.

Brace yourself, Terry, he thought. *This is the storm you've always known was coming.*

And then he waded right in.

"We've come tonight to tell you that Marx and Lenin did not know the way," he had blurted out. "Jesus Christ is the only way. The Bible says he is the way, the truth, and the life, and there is no way to truly live other than to know him.

"I know what it's like to be doing well in college but feel completely unhappy in your heart," he had proclaimed, as the club fell silent. All over the room, the audience of young Polish twenty-somethings had put down their beer and let their cigarettes burn out, and leaned forward in rapt attention.

The looks on their faces had emboldened Terry, and for another ten minutes he had summarized his troubled youth and subsequent surrender to Christ.

"I was drinking to try to cope with my misery, but God saved me. And if he could reach out and touch a drunken college student like me, I know he can do the same thing for you."

Those few minutes had brought Terry both the greatest thrill and most frightening moments of his entire ministry, and after he had walked off stage it had come as no surprise to be taken by the arms and marched into this basement. If anything, he was relieved to be here, rather than a KGB holding cell.

Lord, you said you would send us behind the Iron Curtain, he thought as his heart welled up with praise. *But this is not a secret prayer meeting in someone's apartment. This is—astounding.*

At last, the applause came to an end and Terry looked up at his interrogator, wondering what would happen next. Would he be arrested? Would the team be sent packing back to the border?

The director was starting to speak, when the door at the top of the stairs opened. One by one, the members of Living Sound filed into the room and lined up along the wall. Terry knew they were wondering if they should prepare for the second concert, or pack their bags and get out of town.

"This man is accusing us of being from the CIA," Terry announced after the last team member had entered. A couple of the girls looked nervous, so he tried to sound cheerful.

"I told him we just came to sing, like we were invited to do."

"This cannot continue," interjected the director. "We will not allow it."

"Well, they've got a problem on their hands," said Larry. The grin on Terry's face had emboldened him. "The first crowd is gone and the room is already full, with several hundred more in the square outside still trying to get in. Evidently the word's going all over town about what's happening here tonight."

Terry looked at the team with a *shall we?* expression on his face. All along the wall heads subtly nodded up and down in response. Then Terry turned to the director and squared himself in his chair.

"Sir, we haven't asked you for any payment and we don't want any," said Terry. "But I know you've made a lot of money selling tickets tonight, and those young people upstairs are already filling up on beer. I doubt they're going to be in any kind of a mood for a refund."

God, this is so amazing, thought Terry. *You brought us into a perfect situation we could never have arranged. And you've kept us safe and put our enemies in danger.*

"What's it going to be?" Terry challenged.

He could see that the director had already realized the jam he was in. Now he was huddling with his two cohorts over by the wall opposite the team. After a couple of minutes, he turned and lifted his chin, as if to make a formal announcement.

"You may sing," he said, pointing his index finger along the row at his American guests. Then he turned and pointed at Terry.

"But *you* may not speak. You stay in the back of the room, and do not go near the stage. Do you understand?"

"Yes, sir," replied Terry, with a genuinely pleasant smile. "We'll be happy to comply."

Terry turned and gave the team a telling wink as he nodded them towards the stairs.

This guy has no idea he's making history, he thought. *The Youth Communist Party of Poland has just sold standing-room-only tickets to a revival meeting.*

Fifteen minutes later, Terry parked himself conspicuously beside Joel Vesanen, Living Sound's bus driver, against the back wall of the ancient stone hall that now served the Party's purposes.

Judging from the noise filtering in from the street, Larry had not been exaggerating. The club, which normally seated about a hundred people, was already filled twice over, and what sounded like a crowd of several hundred more were waiting outside on the cold cobblestones of Old Krakow.

At precisely 7 p.m., Living Sound struck up the first song of their second concert. Larry had ditched the pop tunes and gone straight into a raucous old spiritual featuring the brass section and a solo by Jan that immediately set the place hopping.

"This should be fun," Terry yelled, cupping his hand by Joel's ear.

The first song ended and the party's interpreter started to walk onstage, but Larry waved him off and launched into another crowd pleaser.

Way to go, Larry, thought Terry. The interpreter had done his best to twist everything spoken during the first concert, but so many corrections had been yelled from the audience that it had become clear nearly everyone present could understand English. And best of all, they could understand the message of Christ in the songs, which was why he had been so compliant when the director had banned him from the stage.

He has no idea, thought Terry. *He took my pistol, but let us keep our cannons.*

As he listened to song after song, Terry couldn't remember a time when the group had sounded better or been so well-received. He had never seen an audience so completely enthralled, not just by the music, but by the message it carried. That much was obvious from all the thumbs up and elbow jabs every time they heard the name of Jesus.

"To be Polish is to be Catholic" had been a saying centuries before Communism had come along. Maybe that was the key. These students had spent their lives giving prescribed atheistic answers to every question they had ever been asked. But tonight was their chance to be nothing but truly, fully Polish for a few hours, without the empty oaths and insipid socialist slogans that nobody believed anyway.

God, you really are moving by your Spirit, marveled Terry as Living Sound played the introduction to what had suddenly become his favorite song. Most of the team were singing and playing through tears, and they all had their hands raised. He looked around the club. People in the audience were crying too.

I wonder if these students have ever cried like that in their lives, he thought. And what was going to happen to them for doing it now?

The song ended louder than it ever had, and this time the ovation was even more deafening than before, as the audience demanded one encore, and then another, and another. Terry looked for the club's Communist bosses, but they were nowhere to be seen. Had they given up, or did they fear for their own safety? He would probably never know.

Lord, how far will the shock waves from this carry after tonight? Terry wondered, as he flicked a tear from his own cheek. After all, this was *communist* Poland, so it wasn't unthinkable that the news might reach Warsaw.

Had he also guessed "Russia," Terry would not have been wrong.

Yet tonight's collision of creeds would also produce a third wave, one that would reach in a very different direction than Terry could possibly have known. For beneath her veneer of feigned allegiance, the heartstrings of the real Poland stretched south, not east, to the city where, it was said, all roads used to lead. And in the case of Krakow, Poland, tonight's events made that saying a certainty: Living Sound's apparent wrong turn into a Polish communist nightclub would become their road to Rome.

CHAPTER 8

STORM
ON PURPOSE

WHEN TERRY RETURNED HOME with Living Sound in mid-1973, the story of their Polish nightclub concert and Terry's disruptive message took on a life of its own. Before long, they were singing and preaching everywhere from high schools in Florida to Robert Schuller's "Hour of Power" television show in California. Larry Dalton and he had been right: contemporary music was a great vehicle for taking the gospel onto almost any platform anywhere.

Almost.

"Would you like to bring your group to my church this weekend?" asked a Catholic priest the next spring after Living Sound had performed at a Jesuit high school in Tampa, Florida.

Terry glanced at the starched white collar around the priest's neck.

"I'll pray about it," he said, trying to deflect the question. *He's Catholic*, thought Terry. *There's no way I'm going to preach in a Roman Catholic church.*

The priest handed Terry his business card and left. But it didn't matter. Catholics were as lost as Communists. And while it was one thing to preach to sinners, it was quite another to partner with them. After all, hadn't he been taught that both Catholicism and Communism were mentioned in Bible prophecy as being part of the Antichrist's plan to impose a one-world government?

But the priest's invitation wouldn't leave Terry alone, and a few nights later he watched uneasily as Living Sound set up their instruments for a Saturday evening concert at St. Lawrence Catholic Church in downtown Tampa.

The drums look so strange under that big crucifix, thought Terry. *Lord, I don't know if we belong here. Let's just get this over with and leave.*

At 7 p.m., Living Sound settled into their opening set before a capacity crowd.

That's better, thought Terry, after their first song met with enthusiastic applause. After several days of inner tension over his decision, he felt himself relaxing at last. St Lawrence had become just another venue. By the time the team closed forty minutes later with *God is Moving*, he was ready to preach his usual, no-holds-barred challenge to the people to commit their lives to Jesus.

"You may have gone to church all your life," said Terry a few minutes later as he wrapped up his short homily. As always, it was time to feel his way to the right ending.

They were probably all baptized as infants, he thought.

"But there's no substitute for a self-conscious, grownup commitment to Christ. You see, it's one thing to learn about Jesus"—he pointed to the life-size crucifix that hung on the wall behind him—"but it's another thing to really know him. And tonight, if you want to know the Lord Jesus personally, please come and kneel here at the front to ask him for yourself."

Whoa, what's this? Terry wondered, as the whole crowd moved forward. It looked as though he had ordered them to evacuate the pews.

"Please pray for me, sir," said a sobbing teenaged girl, as Terry approached the platform step where she knelt.

"Me, too," said a lady next to her. "This is my daughter, and we both want to know Jesus Christ like you said."

The three-sided platform was ringed four and five deep with kneeling parishioners all wanting prayer. Terry waved the team members over, motioning them to lay their hands on people's shoulders and pray with them. Then, after ministering to the lady and her daughter, he moved along the line, praying with the people kneeling in front of him.

When he had reached the wall where the line ended, Terry looked up and noticed a visiting Irish priest he had met before the concert. The man's brow was wrinkled with emotion, and a moment later he disappeared around the corner into the sacristy, where the priests stored their vestments and the "host," the wine and bread.

See what he needs.

It was just an impression, but Terry obeyed all the same. When he entered, the priest had knelt at a small altar in front of the host, and was praying fervently while fingering his rosary beads. Instinctively, Terry walked up behind the priest and touched him on the shoulder to pray for him.

It was the lightest touch, but suddenly Terry felt something reverberating through his body. The voice from back in Springs, South Africa, was speaking to him once again.

I'm going to take you into the Roman Catholic Church.

As before, the words came from deep within, but this time Terry felt no compulsion to fall on his face. Instead, a vivid scene formed in his mind. There was Living Sound, back behind the Iron Curtain in Poland. Now, they were singing and preaching, not in a nightclub, but in the cavernous Roman Catholic cathedrals they had driven past eighteen months earlier in Krakow.

Lord, I'm not going to question this, Terry silently prayed. *I know it must be from you. But all I've ever heard is how the Catholic Church is a tool of the devil. So I really need your help.*

How does a person shed a lifetime of bias? What do you do when you realize you've believed a lie, but still don't know the truth?

* * *

From his earliest days, Terry had been taught that the Roman Catholic Church was the "Whore of Babylon" mentioned in the Book of Revelation, and that the Pope was the biblical "beast" who would collude with the Antichrist to take over the world. He knew that the rest of his Living Sound team had been taught the same thing.

Terry opened his eyes and looked down at the priest kneeling in front of him. The man was still deep in prayer, and almost childlike in his sincerity. Rosary beads or not, he clearly was seeking with all his heart to know God better.

Then something Jesus had said in Matthew 25 flashed across Terry's mind, and he felt ashamed: "Whatever you do to the least of these, my brothers, you've done it to me."

Lord, I've preached those words, and all the while I was the guilty party, he prayed. *I've rejected these people and never realized I was rejecting you.*

Shame quickly gave way to repentance, and as Terry exited the sacristy to the sight of his musicians packing up their instruments, he knew there was only one course of action to take.

There's no use putting this to a vote, he told himself. *I'd better just do what I did in South Africa four years ago and proclaim it. We're going back to Poland to work among Catholics.*

Two nights later, when the team had finished their concert at a local Methodist church, Terry took to the platform to make the big announcement before his sermon. He felt sure he was doing the right thing, but still wondered whether his Protestant audience would respond or react.

"God spoke to me this past weekend that he's taking Living Sound into the Roman Catholic Church in Poland," he said confidently. "We'll be off to Europe a month from now, and I'm looking forward to seeing what he's going to do."

The Methodist congregation responded with enthusiasm, and as Terry preached, he reassured himself that his fear of controversy had been unfounded. But after the service had ended and the auditorium was empty, the fireworks began. Some members of the team were already threatening to quit and go home.

"Do you believe in praying to Mary?" one of the singers asked in an accusing tone. "Do you believe in praying to the saints, or that the wine actually turns into Jesus' blood?" These were questions Terry had expected people to ask—but not as friendly fire from within the team.

"Look, this is not a doctrinal issue," Terry replied. "It's simply a command from the Lord, so we have to obey it. And it doesn't require any of us to change our beliefs."

The grousing continued for another month, but by the time the team departed for Europe in May 1974, no one had dropped out.

* * *

Northern Europe was in the middle of a beautiful summer six weeks later as Living Sound topped a series of concerts across Europe and Scandinavia with an appearance at Billy Graham's prestigious "Lausanne '74" evangelism conference in Switzerland. Now, they were looking forward to a week off at a castle-turned-ministry retreat in Bavaria.

"When do we land in Germany?" asked one of the team members as their bus pulled aboard their all-night ferry in Trelleborg, Sweden.

"Actually, tomorrow morning we dock in some place in Poland that I can't pronounce, and then we drive west to Germany," replied Don Moen, as he set the brake and climbed out of the driver's seat.

"Did you say Poland?" asked Terry, fumbling to retrieve the boarding pass he had just stuck in his jeans pocket. *Swinoujscie, Poland*, said the stub. He stared at the paper for a moment and then returned it to his pocket.

Could this be our ticket to those cathedrals? Terry wondered. The team had transit visas to get them to the West German border, but they weren't authorized to go anywhere else within Poland. Still, Terry felt an urge to take the team southeast to Warsaw. And if he did, no one would know for at least a couple of days. At least he had until dawn to think it over.

By the time the ferry docked in Poland the next morning, Terry had made up his mind, but waited to speak until Don had pulled the bus onto dry land.

"OK, everybody," he said, holding the tinny-sounding dashboard microphone close to his mouth. "You've all heard about our previous team's nightclub escapade two years ago here in Poland. What do you say we postpone our vacation for a day or so and drive to Warsaw just to see what might happen? The roads are lousy, but I think we can make it by dark."

"Why not?" said one of the band members, yawning. "We might never get to do something like this again."

A chorus of groans followed, more from tired consent than objection.

"This is crazy, Terry," said Don, laughing as he wheeled the bus onto the pothole-riddled main road that led towards Warsaw. "If we get stopped, we're in big trouble."

Don looked up at Terry and then they smiled wryly at one another. The morning sky was clear, but both men knew they were purposely heading into another spiritual storm. In fact, this time they were stirring one up.

More than twelve hours later, as the bus cruised into downtown Warsaw, Terry was on the lookout for two things: churches, and a cheap hotel that wouldn't ask questions.

"Don, stop right here," said Terry, pointing to his right as the bus approached a forced right turn.

"OK," replied Don, pulling to the curb. "But I don't see any hotels around here."

"I know," said Terry. Then he pointed to a pale yellow building dead ahead, where the current street met the pedestrian plaza of Old Town. "But that looks like a church, and I just felt a little nudge inside that we should stop here."

Don parked the bus and the team piled out onto the sidewalk. It felt good to put their feet on the ground and everyone stretched their legs for a minute before following Terry through the tall, narrow doors of historic St. Anne's Church. It was nearing 8:30 p.m. on a Tuesday night, but there were at least a hundred worshipers present.

"Look, everyone's kneeling," whispered Don out of the side of his mouth.

"Good. That's exactly what we need to do too," whispered Terry, as the team filed into a vacant row and knelt on the prayer rails like everyone else. "Let's face it; we're flying by the seat of our pants."

Terry looked up at the ornately frescoed ceiling. The sanctuary seemed even taller than it was wide, and every square inch above the floor had been either meticulously painted or inlaid with gold. Even the confessional booths looked like they were worth more money than any of the church buildings his dad had built in Canada.

Terry lowered his head and began moving his lips.

"Father, we made it, but we're winging it all the way," he prayed. "What in the world do we do now?"

All at once, Terry felt the same gentle nudge as he had felt in the bus.

Start here.

That was it. *Stop here. Start here.* Four words in total. Yet somehow, like matches struck in a pitch-black cavern, they were enough that Terry knew he should keep inching his way along. Sooner or later he would come to a brighter light.

That light came the next morning when Father George Dombrowski, the friendly rector of St. Anne's, welcomed Terry into his study and immediately suggested that Living Sound give a concert following Thursday afternoon's mass.

The next day, two days after they had driven into town on nothing but a hunch, the team began carting their gear up the ancient stone aisles of St. Anne's sanctuary.

"Terry, I feel like we're violating this place," winced Don as he emerged onto the sidewalk for a second piece of equipment. "I never realized the wheels on my guitar amp squeaked so loudly."

"And if one of our loudspeakers tips over, it'll crush something priceless, no matter what direction it falls," chimed in Greg, who played bass.

"It's okay, guys," replied Terry. "I've got a feeling this place is going to fill up, and in an hour we'll be singing to 800 people who've probably never heard the gospel like they're going to hear it today. In the meantime, let's get finished and meet in the sacristy for prayer. We need to be ready."

But there was no way for Terry and the team to be ready for the sight that greeted them at St. Anne's when they exited the sacristy at five o'clock to begin singing. Where once there had been aisles and pews and steps and a nave, now there was nothing but a sea of faces some five to six feet above where the floor had been. There were faces in every direction, smiling, young and tender, old and weathered—countless earnest, eager faces. All of them waiting for whatever sounds this American band would make—they had been told—for the glory of God.

Terry stood in the sacristy doorway and looked at Father George, who was beaming with delight, despite tears in his eyes.

"I told...only today," he said in halting English.

Terry turned to look for a pathway through the crowd. He wanted to get to the back of the sanctuary, his usual vantage point during the music, but couldn't even see the edge of the platform. He looked to his left at Don, who was trying to make eye contact with Wally at the drums in order to start the first song. But where Wally should be, there were only people standing in a circle, looking down. At length, two sticks appeared just above eye level in the center of the circle and clicked off a tempo. Then the first notes sounded and the concert was underway.

Terry ducked back into the sacristy to find some way around the crowd. A second door led him outside, into the courtyard and around the church, where a wall and an old wooden door separated the peaceful, verdant gardens of St. Anne's from the stone-paved bustle of the Old Town plaza.

Terry started to grab for the handle on the door, when a voice behind him gave him a start.

"There is no way to see from outside, my friend," said Father George Dombrowski in heavily accented English. "There are three thousand people inside, and perhaps one thousand more there." He nodded towards the door. "You should come back into the sacristy and wait there."

"This is amazing," said Terry as the priest held the door for his reentry.

"Yes," replied Father George, "and praise to God, it is wonderful."

Just as Terry expected, Living Sound had to satisfy the crowd's demand for encores before he could come out of the sacristy to preach.

Lord, will they even want to hear what I have to say? he worried as he made his way past about twenty people just to get to the microphone. But then he remembered. This was *communist* Poland, and anything an American had to say about God was as welcome here as the best music on earth.

Just as he had back in Tampa, Terry challenged the people to publicly confess their faith in Christ. And again, everyone responded, including the priests.

"Terry, I spent most of tonight's concert repenting while I played bass," confessed Greg as the team packed their gear a couple of hours later. Along with all the others, he had prayed for hundreds of people. "Two days ago I was ready to quit the team before playing in a Catholic church, but tonight I realized I was privileged to be a part of making history. I'm so sorry."

"I know what you mean," said Terry. "I felt the same way a few weeks ago, but here we are. And I think this is just the beginning of something we can't even imagine."

As he spoke those words, Terry remembered the verse from First Corinthians that he had personalized and endlessly repeated years earlier during his week-long fast back in Medicine Hat.

"Eye has not seen, nor ear heard, nor have entered into my heart the things which you have prepared for those who love you."

Then a thought struck him, as though a cartoon-style light bulb had clicked on above his head.

It never entered into your heart, because your heart was closed. Stay open, Terry. Stay open.

The next morning there was a knock on Terry's door. It was Father George.

"His Eminence, Stefan Cardinal Wyszynski, would like to meet you and your team," he said, with a look of pride on his face. "He has heard about your ministry at our church, and he wishes to receive you to give you his blessing,"

Terry had learned about the Cardinal in his studies over the past few weeks, and relayed what he knew to the team later that day.

"Cardinal Wyszynski was in prison for nearly four years during the 1950s," he told them. "He and the younger Cardinal, Karol Wojtyla, are the two most respected men in Poland. If he gives us his blessing, there's no telling what could happen."

The next morning, Father George guided Living Sound's bus to the massive Primate's Palace, and then led the team into a large, columned reception hall with parquet flooring. The cardinal lived in more humble surroundings, he explained, and only used the palace for special occasions.

Within minutes a protocol officer signaled that the cardinal was arriving, and Terry quickly formed the team into a circle as he had been instructed. A moment later a white-haired man wearing red robes and a matching red miter atop his head entered and began shaking each team member's hand.

Lord, this man carries real authority, thought Terry, as the cardinal made his way along. *It's not just the robes. Something more than a ceremony is happening here.*

At length his Eminence came to Terry and paused, while a translator whispered something in his ear. Then he smiled broadly and placed his hands on Terry's shoulders.

"May the anointing of Augustine and Jerome dwell upon your declaration of the word of God," said the cardinal in English.

A familiar feeling swept over Terry at that moment, and instinctively he bowed his head and closed his eyes.

Father, what's happening? he inwardly prayed, before realizing when he had felt this way before. It was the same feeling of impartation he had felt years earlier, on the cold Oklahoma morning when Oral Roberts had touched his shoulders and blessed his ministry to the nations. It was the transmittal of authority.

The cardinal spoke again, and Terry raised his head to look him in the eyes.

"I was told about your ministry at St. Anne's," he said. "The communists control our country. They tell our young people that God is dead, but you have a message of life, and to you God is not dead. You are an example to the young people of all of Poland. I open every basilica, cathedral, and church to you. You may minister anywhere with our blessing to bring your message to the nation of Poland."

Only four days ago, Terry had followed a spiritual whim and turned the team bus south, into the heart of a country whose government only wanted them gone. But somehow God had guided them, step by step, to the hands that held the real power in Poland—hands whose touch only weeks ago Terry would have disdained the way ancient Jews scorned Samaritans. Hands that had just given him the keys to a whole nation.

* * *

If ever there had been a perfect storm in his life, Terry faced one when he returned to Poland with Living Sound in the autumn of 1974. Cardinal Wyszynski's blessing had opened every church in the country to the team's ministry, and neither the Communist government nor any potentially antagonistic bishop could oppose such power. Even better, the spiritual coup that the group had pulled off at the Communist nightclub in Krakow two years earlier had given them spectacular advance publicity. Church attendance in the already-religious country rose dramatically everywhere they went.

Eventually the crowds coming to hear Living Sound outgrew even the largest cathedrals, and in some cities up to 20,000 people jammed the streets while Terry and the teams sang and preached from makeshift platforms built by the priests and townsfolk. It was obvious that in keeping his promise to open Poland's churches, Cardinal Wyszynski had opened the nation's heart as well.

Still, nothing in all his years of ministry there could have prepared Terry for the sight that greeted him in 1976, when he stepped onstage before nearly 300 thousand people at a festival in Czestochowa and saw a childhood prophecy come to pass.

I see you standing before a large crowd of people someday...You've got a Bible in your hand.

This is what McLaughlin saw, Lord. This is it, thought Terry, looking at the Bible in his hand as he stepped to the microphone to preach. For a moment he was fourteen years old again, sitting in the dark, in the back of the tabernacle at Nanoose Bay.

God help me. This is the vision. This is why I'm alive.

Terry surveyed the crowd, which extended a quarter mile to either side. It was time to preach.

"We have come today to honor Mary, the mother of Jesus," he began, "because the Holy Bible says that all generations shall call her blessed."

Then Terry turned to the second chapter of John, and read the story of the wedding where Jesus turned water into wine.

"Listen to what the Lord's mother said when the wine had run out and the servants asked her for help: 'Do whatever my son tells you.' That was her wish, and today it remains what she says to all who would seek her help. 'Do whatever my son tells you.'

"And what does Jesus, the son of Mary and the son of God, tell us to do? He tells us that we must be born again."

Standing there on the balcony of an ancient monastery, looking out over an honest-to-goodness "sea" of souls, Terry felt himself more alive than ever before. And if he were honest with himself, purposely taking that wrong turn from the ferry and heading for Warsaw two years earlier hadn't really been a hunch. It had been a confident first step in the dark, the kind that can only be made by someone whose experience assures him that the light comes *after* that step, not before. And here it was.

This is perfect, Lord, he marveled more than once as he preached. *It's a perfect day in a perfect setting. And this is exactly the right Scripture for these people. How could it get any better?*

Terry glanced over at Cardinal Wojtyla. The team's influential patron was beaming from ear to ear—a sure sign that things would get better. Like a hurricane in warm waters, Living Sound's perfect storm in Poland was growing even larger.

Stay open, Terry. Stay open.

CHAPTER 9

THE EVIL EMPIRE

BY 1977, TERRY WAS DEPLOYING three, fulltime Living Sound teams around the world, and considering a fourth. Yet for all his success, from Warsaw to Vietnam to Venezuela, he longed to return to Soviet Estonia, to taste again the fellowship he had found at an underground prayer meeting years earlier.

He had made a vow on that dangerous night.

"If God ever calls me to come back, I will. No matter what, I'll come."

Now, nearly ten years later, Terry knew it was time to fulfill his vow. And since his ministry's plate was already full, he made the decision to expand again.

In March 1978, Living Sound 4 kicked off its inaugural tour in England, then gradually sang its way to Helsinki, Finland, where the team boarded the same ferry that had taken Terry to Estonia a decade earlier.

But an old question remained: How could a large Christian concert ensemble simply cruise into a country where believers often had to meet in secret just to pray? The answer came with one look at the secondhand bus Living Sound had purchased for the new team. The coach's previous owners had used it to cart tourists around England, and the banner script on its sides still advertised *Home James Tours.*

"Let's name it *Home James*," suggested a team member. "Let's leave the sign as is, and let the Soviet immigration authorities assume we're a band on vacation."

The idea worked like a charm, and in early May, Terry found himself back in the USSR, peering through the window of his hotel room at the weathered doors and faded white walls of the Tallinn Methodist Church, half a block away. The last time he had seen the place it was surrounded by armed Soviet troops.

Will we have to sneak around like the last time, Lord? Terry wondered as he surveyed the streets below. *Or will you do something incredible here like you've done in Poland?*

But unlike Poland, the Soviet Union had no powerful cardinal who could defy her dictators to open the way. There was only the little Methodist church nearby, a larger Baptist church in the center of Old Town, and—Terry hoped—his friend, Jon.

A day of door knocking ensued, and Jon was still nowhere to be found, but the Baptist pastor did offer to host an unannounced evening concert. Word quickly spread, and by nightfall on Living Sound's second day in the country, more than a thousand people were jammed into the lofty, stone sanctuary of Ole Vista Church in Old Tallinn.

As the music began, Terry headed for his usual perch at the back of the hall. This time it wasn't the sound that concerned him, but keeping an eye out for the KGB. There was no way that a church in the USSR could be filled to capacity on a weeknight without the government finding out. Before long, however, he realized that even if there were spies present, they had decided to let the meeting proceed. He might have to face them later, but for now, Living Sound was in the clear.

Just as in Poland, the response here was overwhelming, although it came more through weeping than applause. Terry looked across the crowd and noticed a teary-eyed young blond woman, sitting on the center aisle a couple of rows from the back.

She looks familiar, thought Terry. *Wait—that's Mae, the girl who prayed so passionately ten years ago at Jon's secret meeting.*

Terry walked to Mae's row and knelt beside her, cupping his hand by her ear.

"Why are you crying?" he whispered, hoping she had learned English. She had, and her reply took him by surprise.

"Our youth group heard Living Sound sing on Polish radio three years ago," Mae whispered, "and we have been praying ever since that God would bring you to Estonia. I am crying because at last you are really here!"

Terry was still reeling from Mae's words after the concert, when he walked into the prayer room and straight into a bear hug from a grinning Jon Karner. The black, bushy hair and beard, the broad smile, the eyes more than a little mischievous—ten years had not changed Jon at all.

The two men pulled up chairs and quickly began catching up. They were both married now. Jon had two sons—Terry two girls and a boy. Jon had worked several jobs, but his first love was still illegal youth ministry, even though it meant frequent KGB raids on his home. Terry started to share a little of Living Sound's history, but Jon stopped him.

"I know about the group," he said. "Living Sound is well known among Christian young people not just in Estonia, but all over the USSR. Even now, a group of Russian believers more than

2,000 miles to our east is boarding a train to come to Tallinn, because the news is already spreading that you are here."

Jon's words staggered Terry, and for a moment he felt like he was back in Krakow, Poland, when the town square had swarmed with young people rushing to hear Living Sound.

Here we go again, thought Terry as his pulse quickened. But his excitement was quickly tempered, as Jon continued.

"Once the KGB decided five black cars would follow me around the city," Jon said. "They drive big cars called Volgas, like your Chevrolets. They followed me everywhere for a whole day, with three men in each car, and parked outside my house when I went home. Often a smaller car with many antennas sits all night outside my house. My neighbors are paid to spy on me, and sometimes down the street I see long microphones pointing at our windows. I cannot even teach my sons about God unless I turn the radio up very loud."

Terry's heart grew heavy as he imagined his own family having to live under such pressure.

"They have burst into my home many times looking for Bibles, but every time God gives me a dream the night before and I hide everything. They have never caught me, but still, the click of a Volga's door can wake me from my sleep."

Spying on him all the time...frequent KGB raids on his home... Lord, don't let me make any foolish moves, prayed Terry. He had thought about danger to himself and the team, but now he saw what the slightest mistake might cost this man and his family.

Terry and Jon talked until almost 10 p.m., and then agreed to meet again at a safe location the next afternoon.

"Hold onto your hats, guys," Terry told the team on the short ride back to their hotel. "I've got a feeling something big is about to pop. But it could get dangerous, and not only for us."

How would they make their way through what was clearly a viper pit of spies and informants?

* * *

The Hotel Viru was where most American tourists stayed. "At least the ones worth spying on," Jon had said back at the church. "The 23rd floor is KGB only. From there they aim long-distance listening devices around the city. Also, most of the rooms have microphones built into televisions, radios, and even the ceiling sprinklers."

Although Terry suspected that the hotel's restaurant was also bugged, the adrenalin rush of the past few hours had spiked the team's appetites and he knew they needed to eat and unwind. Everyone headed to the restaurant, which doubled as a club at night. The presence of a good jazz ensemble made for a welcome wrap-up to a tense day.

"That woman's a really good singer," whispered Randy, the team's leader.

"Yeah, her name's Marju," replied Roger, the drummer. "Jon says she's famous all over the Soviet Union. Singing in a tourist hotel is the most prestigious gig you can get here."

The team had arrived midway through Marju's set, and soon it was time for her break.

Roger leaned across the table. "Hey Terry, mind if we introduce ourselves to the band?" he asked.

"Go ahead," said Terry, smearing unsalted butter on a piece of black bread. "Let's see what happens."

Terry watched as Roger, David, and Gary, the sax player, strode over to the edge of the stage to say hello.

"Drums," said Roger, pointing at himself and flicking his wrists up and down.

"Guitar," said David, strumming the air.

"Saxophone," added Gary. "American band."

Marju had started toward the kitchen, but turned around at the word, *American*.

"Oh, you must play!" she said in throaty, accented English.

She looks like she's lived a hard life, thought Terry as he watched from his seat thirty feet away. Marju had a drink in her hand, but she appeared quite pleased at whatever the guys were saying.

Terry took a bite of beef stroganoff while his musicians made a beeline back to his table.

"Terry, they want us to play!" said Gary.

Again, Terry thought back to the club in Krakow, and to his upbraiding by the Communist authorities.

We could get into some real hot water for this, he told himself.

Isn't that why I brought you here? said a familiar inner voice.

"Do it, guys," he said, bracing himself for a potentially long night.

Living Sound took the stage and straightaway sang several songs about Jesus, before Marju came back for her final set of the night. A few nervous diners got up and left, but again, no authorities showed themselves.

So where's the hot water? thought Terry, when the show ended at midnight. Now he was troubled by the lack of opposition. Something was not right.

* * *

Shortly after lunch the next day, a teenaged boy approached Terry just outside the Viru's entrance.

"I am Peeter, Mae's brother," said the boy in a cordial voice. "Jon sent me to tell you that the church is full of people waiting for your band to come. He says that you are big news all over Tallinn because you sang about Jesus last night in the hotel. He says the police are angry, but they probably will not stop you if you come to our church." The boy nodded towards the Methodist church a short distance away.

Terry thanked Peeter, and as discreetly as he could he mustered the group onto *Home James* and headed down the street to unload the instruments.

Just like the big church in Old Town, the little Methodist building was packed to twice its capacity, with Marju and her band occupying most of the front row, just as they would every time Living Sound appeared for the remainder of their brief visit.

Six days after entering the Soviet Union, Terry and the team returned to Finland, leaving behind a Soviet city already clamoring for their return. Marju had accepted Christ, and news of her conversion and healing from alcoholism was already causing a sensation.

How long would it be, Terry wondered, before the KGB realized what a sizable hole his "band on vacation" had just punched in their fabled Iron Curtain?

* * *

As Terry pulled into his driveway back in Tulsa a few days later, seven-year-old Misty and four-year-old Scot bounded out the front door of his house to greet him, followed a moment later by Jan, who was cradling five-month-old Rebecca in her arms.

Terry kissed his wife, and pulled the baby into his arms while Misty and Scot tugged at his waist. His life had become so rich and full over the past year. For one thing, his dad Bert had retired from the ministry and spent months renovating the old house Terry had bought on 91st Street. Then Becca had been born in March, right before Living Sound's breakthrough trip to Tallinn. And topping everything off, their ministry in Poland continued to explode, spilling over into other predominately Catholic regions from Spain to northern Ireland.

How could a man's life get any better? he asked himself as he walked into the house.

The answer came two months later on October 16th, when on a warm afternoon in Rome, Terry's friend, Cardinal Wojtyla, became Pope John Paul II.

It was a little past noon when the news reached Terry in Minnesota, where he was preaching for a large conference of Catholics caught up in a worldwide movement called the Charismatic Renewal.

"David, send me every album and publicity piece we have in stock," he told his Tulsa office manager by phone that afternoon. "And more business cards. These people know the new pope is a fan of our music, and they're already buying everything and extending invitations."

Was this truly God's plan unfolding? Was it possible that this Polish pope would open the doors to the entire Roman Catholic world for Living Sound to evangelize?

* * *

For the next year, Terry was firing on all cylinders, jetting from team to team all over the globe. At times guilt gripped him. He felt like he was spending more time in Poland than with Jan and the kids back home. But what else could he do? He had to catch every wave and ride out every storm. And lately, the blessing had become a tsunami.

"I just got a message from Jon," Terry's assistant, Joel, told him one afternoon in early 1979. "He wants not only to print Bibles, but also set up a secret recording studio, so he can distribute audio Bibles and Christian music too."

Terry thought back to 1968, when Jon was collecting tinfoil chewing-gum wrappers for a makeshift press. Surely there must be a way to give him something better.

"Randy says Team 4 has found some lead printing plates and are ready to take them in," said Joel. "They're heavy, but we could line the insides of our loudspeakers with them, and as long as the border guards don't take them apart we're fine," said Joel.

In October, fourteen months after their first foray into the USSR, Terry and Living Sound drove through Berlin, and through East Germany to the Soviet Ukraine, where their border crossing came off without a hitch. But now came the real danger.

The transfer would take place at a Baptist church in the forested outskirts of the Ukrainian capital of Kiev. After the uproar caused by Living Sound's ministry in Tallinn the previous year, Terry and Jon both knew that the team would be followed everywhere they went.

"The woods around the church will provide cover," Jon had reassured Terry. "And my friends there have never been in trouble, so the KGB won't suspect them.

"Viktor will also be there to translate," he said. "He is not afraid. He will meet you before the Sunday evening meeting."

"Viktor" was Terry's code name for another Estonian friend he had met in Tallinn. And Viktor had already been in trouble for working with Jon.

Terry and the team left their hotel in Kiev early on a Sunday morning, and by that afternoon they were driving through a peach orchard into the forest where the church sat. Terry walked to the front of the bus and picked up the driver's microphone.

"OK everybody, keep your eyes open. Jon told me the KGB knows we're coming, so until we're sure the coast is clear we only move the small stuff like guitars. If they do show up, we ought to see their dust on this dirt road in plenty of time to act."

Home James pulled up in front of the church and came to a stop. Five minutes passed and nothing happened. Terry looked back at the dirt road. No dust.

"OK, go," he said, and the band members began hustling the loudspeakers from the bins under the bus and into the church, where they carried them to the basement and removed the lead plates. The plates made them three times heavier, and Terry was relieved that no one was around to see his guys wheezing their way up the church steps into the building.

Once the contraband had made it through the door, Terry hiked a quarter mile into the nearby woods to meet Jon, and tell him where the plates were hidden.

"It's all in the basement," said Terry as soon as he saw his friend. There was no time for greetings. "We brought the tape duplicators too, so you're all set."

"The pastor gave me a key yesterday," said Jon. "My friends and I will come back late tonight and take everything to Tallinn. Thank you, Terry."

The two men hugged and Terry walked back through the woods to the clearing by the church, before stopping in his tracks. He had been gone for only ten minutes, but during that time a

KGB van had pulled up and parked no more than 20 feet from where he stood.

Keep calm, he told himself, and then hiked his belt and checked his zipper, as if he had gone into the woods for a different reason.

Inwardly, Terry felt a thrill that the agents in the van seemed oblivious to what was happening right under their noses. They offered no reaction when Viktor appeared a few minutes before the concert, and then sat peacefully during the music and Terry's sermon, before tailing the team back to their hotel later that night.

Good, thought Terry. *Now it will be a lot easier for Jon to retrieve the equipment from the church.*

Back in his room that night, Terry tried to sleep, but something Roger had told him after the service kept him awake.

"A man in a suit came up to me while we were packing up our gear," Roger had said, "and he told me that they know our name is Living Sound, and that we're trouble makers and we're going to go to jail."

They're coming, aren't they Lord? Terry prayed. *They've been watching this whole time and now they're coming.*

By the middle of the night, Terry was sure that a confrontation lay ahead in the morning. What would he say? Would there be handcuffs? What if they had found Jon or taken Viktor?

A passage from Acts chapter 4 entered Terry's mind then. He had read it several times the past few months, and the words came easily.

"Whether it is right in the sight of God to listen to you rather than to God, you must judge, for we cannot but speak of what we have seen and heard."

That's it, Lord, he prayed. *We're here because we listened to you, so that's what we'll keep doing.*

Terry sighed with relief when Viktor walked into the dining room the next morning during breakfast, but his friend wore a stone face, and looked as though he hadn't slept.

"Sit down and have something to eat," said Terry, as if he didn't know what was coming.

Viktor kept standing.

"There are some people who wish to speak with you," he said. "You need to follow me."

Terry rose to his feet and followed his friend down the hall. Then Viktor stopped, and pointed him into a room, before parking himself against the corridor wall.

The room was gray and unadorned, save for starkly colored portraits of Vladimir Lenin and Soviet leader Leonid Brezhnev. In the room's center, a man clad in dull green military garb sat behind a desk, flanked by armed soldiers. In the corner to Terry's right sat another man in a suit as plain as the walls. But the look of deference on the officer's face made it clear who was in charge.

KGB, thought Terry without a trace of doubt or—to his surprise—fear.

"You know you are going to jail, don't you?" demanded the man at the desk. "You have broken many Soviet laws, and your whole group can be detained."

"We haven't broken any laws," replied Terry calmly.

The lack of fear in his voice seemed to antagonize the officer.

"Yes, you have broken our laws and you *will* go to jail!" repeated the officer. Then he justified his accusation with some oblique reference to rules governing tourist activity.

Terry started to answer, but decided to hold his tongue until the man ran out of steam.

Ten minutes later, the officer finally paused.

Maybe he's gone through his whole manual, Terry thought, and then he felt his spine stiffen. He'd had enough.

"Sir, Article 52 of your constitution specifically says your citizens are guaranteed freedom of conscience," said Terry. "They have the right to profess or not profess any religion, and to conduct religious worship. That's exactly what we've done. We haven't broken any laws, and we're going to continue visiting churches throughout the Soviet Union."

Good Lord, where did that come from? thought Terry. He had read that article before, but had made no effort to memorize it.

Suddenly, the KGB agent leapt off his chair and shook his fist.

"You are interfering in our domestic affairs," he raged. "We will not allow it!"

"This is religious, not political," replied Terry. "We're going to continue exercising our rights in your country, and the only way you'll stop us *is* to put me in jail."

Then he turned back to the officer.

"Gentlemen, that's all I have to say."

As soon as he had closed the door behind him, Terry's strength forsook him. There was fog forming before his eyes, and he leaned against the wall to keep from passing out.

Viktor placed a steadying hand on his shoulder. "I cannot believe what just happened. You walked out on the KGB. No one does that."

"Let's get out of here," said Terry as his balance returned.

Living Sound quickly checked out of the hotel and headed south towards Tbilisi, Georgia.

"It will be safer to leave you behind for a few days while things cool off," Terry told Viktor. "I might be called in again while we're down south. We can just meet you next week when we return to Tbilisi."

Viktor reluctantly agreed, and the team dropped him off in Tbilisi before continuing south to Armenia for a week of concerts in Yerevan.

* * *

Just as Terry expected, the KGB showed themselves conspicuously everywhere the team went. There were no more confrontations, but somehow, in his gut, he knew a big one was coming.

A week later Terry and Viktor met secretly in a Tbilisi subway station, barely eluding a squad of men who jumped onto a train they thought the two had boarded.

"Have everyone on the bus at 5:30," said Viktor. "I will be fifty meters up the sidewalk, wearing a white hat, and will hail a taxi to lead you to the church."

Terry went back to the hotel and gathered his team leaders in his seventh floor room to fill them in on the plan. He had already been threatened at check-in that morning, and knew that his room would be monitored, so he ran the bathtub faucet at full blast to conceal the conversation.

"Terry, stop," said his sound man, Craig, who was standing on a chair looking up at the ceiling. "Look at this," he mouthed as he pointed to two wires he had just cut. Just as Jon had said back in Tallinn, a microphone had been concealed in the fire sprinkler.

"Out here," motioned Terry, as he led his men out onto the balcony, before continuing in a whisper.

"We're supposed to be on the bus at five-thirt...*get down!*"

Terry yelled. "Someone's pointing a gun at us."

Everyone stopped and stared through the iron railing at a car parked seven stories below.

"It's not a gun," whispered Terry's team leader, Ted. "It's a parabolic microphone. *They're still listening.*"

"Okay, let's meet on the bus at a quarter past five," said Terry in a normal voice as he walked back into his room, and dismissed the gathering. "See you later."

At 5:15, the team went downstairs and began boarding the Living Sound bus, only to discover four additional black cars with four men per car lined up along the curb behind it.

"Wait for me," said Terry to his driver. "I'll be right back."

Volgas, just like the ones Jon described, he said to himself. *They're trying to scare us.*

But Terry was anything but scared. In fact, he felt furious. Still steaming from the afternoon rifle episode, he walked to the car up front and sarcastically saluted the lead agent, the same man who had threatened him that morning at check-in, and then boarded the bus.

Soon Viktor appeared in his white hat further up the block and got into a cab, and the bus eased into the traffic to follow, the KGB cars trailing closely behind.

"I don't think Viktor saw the cars," said Gary. "He doesn't know we've got such a long tail this time."

"Just be ready," ordered Terry, with a little regret in his voice. "I think I just made them mad."

A few minutes later, the entourage pulled up to the church, where Viktor hopped out of his taxi and quickly boarded the bus.

"Did you see those cars?" asked Terry.

"Not until a moment ago," replied Viktor. "What shall I do?"

"Just get into the church as quickly as you can, and if they come after you, we'll stall them," said Terry. It wasn't much of a plan, but what else could he do?

Viktor stepped through *Home James'* folding door, and as soon as his feet touched the sidewalk, the doors of the four Volgas opened and the agents began charging after him.

"Get out and block the sidewalk!" shouted Terry.

In a flash, every guy on the team piled through the door and across the sidewalk, peppering the pursuing agents with random questions. It worked long enough for Viktor to run into the church's courtyard, and a moment later Terry followed him in, a mixture of American chatter and Russian curses fading behind him outside the old iron gates.

Now on safer ground, the pastor and Viktor were talking as Terry approached.

"Pastor, I realize the situation you're in," said Terry. "This morning the KGB showed me a cancellation letter bearing your signature, but I wasn't sure it was real."

"It isn't," replied the pastor. "Do you know how long we have prayed for you to come? We heard about you last year when you were in Tallinn, and we have waited since then for this night. So if you do not care what happens to you, I do not care what happens to me."

"Wait a moment, sir," said Terry apologetically. "I'll be right back."

Terry walked back over to the iron gate.

"Okay, Randy," he called to his road manager. "Bring it all in."

The concert began at the appointed hour, and as usual, the church was full to overflowing with young people, despite the fact that the entire squad of KGB agents had decided to make their presence felt by filling the back row.

It was nearing eight o'clock when Terry began to preach, keenly aware that if ever he had been in danger of having a meeting shut down, this was the night. He looked at the back row, and braced himself when he saw the lead agent sneering at him.

How long, Lord? Terry wondered as he opened his Bible. He looked to his right at Viktor, who gave a resolute nod, and then began to preach.

Terry was barely five minutes into his message when the entire cadre of KGB agents stood and marched up the center aisle, directly toward him. A moment later, they passed the front row and fanned out across the church, stopping no more than fifteen feet away.

Terry was shaken for a moment, but kept preaching, and tried not to lose his train of thought. But a question invaded his mind even as his lips spoke something else.

What now, God? What do I do now?

In years past, Terry had asked that question more often as a man in need of direction than one who already had it. But not this time. "Having done all...stand," St. Paul had said in the Bible, and Terry had come to that point. He had done exactly what God had directed him to do, and now the question was just that of a good soldier checking in. In the meantime, he would keep preaching.

Suddenly, without a word, the lead agent snapped to attention and raised his hand in a formal salute, as if to return the one Terry had given him in front of the hotel.

Terry gave a slight gasp, and the congregation wore a look of amazement, as the row of persecutors turned on their heels and walked out of the side door of the church.

Terry finished his sermon, and after the meeting took Viktor aside to say goodbye. The next morning he would return to Tulsa, while Viktor and the team headed north for Leningrad, 1,700 miles away.

"Viktor, you really need to be careful in the near future," cautioned Terry. "Tonight they held back, but I think that sooner or later they're going to come for you. Your life is in danger."

"I died the day I gave my life to Jesus," said Viktor quietly. "They cannot kill me again. And really, this is the only way I can help my country, so I will continue."

* * *

Six months later, Viktor was arrested, and sentenced to the first of his two years in prison.

CHAPTER 10

IF I MAKE MY BED
IN HELL

THE DRONE OF THE JET ENGINES had a lulling effect. Terry was somewhere over the Atlantic, headed for England, in the early morning hours of Tuesday, September 28, 1982. In the seat beside him, David Weir was dozing. Terry wasn't looking forward to the major restructuring of Living Sound's U.K. office, which David was taking over. Though he knew he needed sleep badly, his mind was churning.

Lord, how could things have started so well in the Soviet Union only to have so many near-disasters befall us since then? he wondered. *You're the one who cleared the way for our work there in the first place. I just don't understand.*

Shutting his eyes, Terry could almost plot the curious rise and fall of his ministry on a graph.

The two years following Living Sound's first foray into Estonia in 1978 had seen the ministry hit peak after peak. The teams had branched out into other parts of the Soviet Union with great success. Jon's underground printing and tape duplication in Estonia were up and running and the spiritual awakening Living Sound had stirred amongst young people there had grown widespread enough to attract the attention of the international press. Terry was even invited by Pope John Paul II to bring Living Sound to the Vatican in August 1980 to sing at one of his Wednesday audiences in St. Peter's Square.

Terry had been so proud for Jan to meet the Pope. After all her sacrifice over the past few years, doing double-time with the kids while he was constantly jetting into the unknown. Of all the missions he could have wished to share with her, seeing her there, being embraced by the most beloved man in the world, was the best gift he could have given her.

The day had provided no less than Terry's own crowning moment, when John Paul had laid his hands on him and blessed him. A million thoughts had flashed through his mind while the Pope prayed. His past prejudices, and the priest's invitation he had almost rejected six years earlier in Tampa. The calling to Roman Catholics that had come when he had touched an Irish priest's shoulder. All the mixed reactions from his Pentecostal friends, when they found out. Cardinal Wyszynski's blessing later that year and Living Sound's amazing ministry in Poland since then. And those two sacred minutes in prayer on the Vatican platform had been the capstone.

There was no doubt about it. Sitting here on the plane more than two years later, Terry could see clearly that the team's ministry with the Pope had been their high point, and that Viktor's imprisonment five months earlier had actually been a portent of the steep slide downward they had experienced ever since.

Viktor's suffering had left Terry deeply shaken. He himself had faced opposition and a degree of danger in the past, but now a good friend had just spent two years in prison because of working with him. He felt guilty, and out of his depth.

Then, six months ago, a recession had hit the American

economy, and the ministry had plunged into a major money crisis. Living Sound's annual operating budget was nearing $1 million at the time, and donations had dropped by fifty percent almost overnight.

Terry still smarted at the memory of having to lay off close friends, not to mention going without his own paycheck for three months. Coming home from overseas to find Jan in tears because the refrigerator was empty—that moment had been the worst of all. In fact, it still was.

What kind of a husband am I? he asked himself, shifting in his seat to try and ward off soreness from the long flight. *And what kind of businessman?*

He thought again of Viktor, sleeping in a cold, filthy cell night after night.

Am I even fit for ministry?

And the problems were still piling up. Now the office in England was in disarray and board members were threatening to resign if Terry didn't step in to make changes.

The sun was beginning to rise outside the plane, when drowsiness finally settled over him.

Lord, help me to solve this mess quickly, so we can get back to your business, he prayed. Yet, as he drifted in and out of a fitful sleep, a half-formed question surfaced in Terry's mind: Had he done something wrong to bring on all this upheaval?

Two hours later, when staff members met Terry and David at Heathrow Airport in London, the question was forgotten. Yet, somewhere within him, an uneasiness remained, like a dirty film in an unwashed glass.

Finally, after the two-hour drive to Living Sound's headquarters in the southwest of England, Terry sat in the parlor with David and a couple of staff members, along with Jim and Dolly Gilbert, who had flown in from Tulsa a few days earlier. It felt good to relax with friends after his long flight, although the hum of the conversation was making him sleepy. Strangely, at about 9 p.m., something felt so wrong.

Thoughts glanced through Terry's head. *I wonder what Jan and the kids are doing.* Then, *Maybe I don't need to fire any more staff after all.* His head felt jumbled.

"If you folks will excuse me, I think I'll go upstairs and hit the sack," said Terry. Tomorrow could take care of itself. Right now, he just wanted to sleep.

The guest room in the former convent was sparsely furnished. Turning off the single bare bulb in the ceiling, Terry crawled wearily into the bottom bunk bed. Everything felt so heavy—his arms, his eyes, his heart. Pulling the covers up to his chin, he shut his eyes and rolled over to face the wall. Sleep came quickly...

Someone was shaking him. *What?*

Terry woke groggily, blinking into the light. The clock showed 11 p.m.; he had been asleep for less than two hours. He looked up. David Weir was the one shaking him, urgently repeating his name.

"Terry. Terry, wake up. You've got to wake up."

David looked as if he'd been crying.

"Terry, we've just received some terrible news." Then his voice broke. "Don called from Tulsa... Jan has been killed in a car accident."

Terry's eyes widened and he looked around the room. There was Jim Gilbert, standing by the light switch. His eyes were brimming with tears.

"Leave me alone you guys," Terry murmured. A heaviness was trying to engulf, but he fought it off. "This is just a stupid dream."

He started to roll back onto his pillow, away from the light.

David caught his shoulder. "No, Terry. Listen to me. I wish it were a dream, but it's not. Jan's been killed."

Slowly, Terry swung his feet to the edge of the bed and sat motionless, staring at his bare feet. Why were there tears, stinging his eyes?

"No. That's not right, David. It's not possible...that can't happen!"

Pressure hit his chest, and jolts of pain. Terry grabbed the springs of the bunk above him and squeezed until the wires dug into his fingers. Reality came thundering in.

"*No!*" he shouted. "*God! This can't be!*"

For a long time he wept.

"Is there a chance you're wrong, David? That she's not dead?" he pleaded.

No.

"When did it happen?"

About two hours ago, around nine our time.

"Where?"

A quarter-mile from the office. None of the children was with her.

"Who are they with?" Gordon and Stella Calmeyer.

"Oh God, my children. Their mother's gone and I'm on the other side of the world. I have to talk to them. Get Gordon on the phone."

* * *

Other than the heartbreaking call to his kids, the rest of that night and the trip home to Tulsa were a blur of anguish. Pain beat at his ribs and in his temples. The words of Jonah came to him.

I have been banished from your sight...the deep surrounds me... But I, with a song of thanksgiving, will sacrifice to you.

He hid his head beneath a pillow. The words were ridiculous. *God, I'll never be able to praise you again.*

Friends met him at the Tulsa airport on Wednesday: Gordon, Joel, Gene Eland and Dr. Ervin, both advisors from his days at ORU. Their embraces were all but lost on him. Nothing mattered except feeling Misty, Scott, and Becca wrap their arms around him when he dropped to his knees in the Calmeyers' living room. He looked into their lost, wounded faces, wishing all of their pain could be heaped into him.

The bitterest part was going home—the absence of Jan's bright greeting when he opened the door. In the living room, he felt a warmth and smelled—what? The vague scent of Jan's favorite cologne lingering in the air. He carried his suitcase upstairs and stopped at the door of their room. On Jan's dresser were a few of her things: her brush, her Bible, a card he'd sent. He couldn't go in.

His house was filled with out-of-town family that night, but it might as well have been deserted for the terrifying loneliness he felt. Only the exhaustion of nearly sixty hours with no sleep drove him into his empty bed.

On Thursday morning, Terry's dad Bert arrived from Canada, with Lorne and Lois, and his old Bible-school friend, Brian Stiller, now head of Youth for Christ in Canada.

"Brian—Dad. I've got to know what happened. Would you take a drive with me?"

Brian drove past Terry's office on 101st Street and continued down the long hill, heading west, the way Jan would have been driving on her way to pick up Becca from preschool. At the bottom of the hill was a narrow bridge over a stream. The sun would have been directly in her eyes, which was why the police supposed her car had drifted to the right until the tires caught on the shoulder. A driver who had been coming the other way reported that Jan had put her hand over her eyes, as though blocking the sun or brushing back her hair. When the car's tires had caught the shoulder, Jan had apparently jerked the wheel to the left to get back into her lane, but her car had careened across the road into a field, flipping end over end as it glanced off an earthen dam by the stream.

Brian pulled off onto the gravel shoulder, where Jim was already waiting. He had gone ahead and surveyed the scene.

Terry climbed out of the car and stumbled down the weedy embankment, with the three men following. Wading through the deep grass, still wet with dew, he saw fresh-turned dirt in the roadside ditch. It had acted like a ski jump, rocketing Jan's car up into the air. Twenty yards beyond, he could see the gouge her front bumper had made in the embankment by the stream.

"Here, Terry," someone called.

Terry looked up and saw Jim standing further out in the field. Walking past pieces of chrome and shattered glass, he came to where Jim was pointing at the ground. He looked and saw two broken ammonia packets, and...he bent down and touched the soil.

Bert and Brian came up from behind. "What is it?"

Unable to answer, Terry held up his hand to reveal a dark red stain on his thumb and forefinger: Jan's blood.

For long minutes, he knelt in the weeds and wept inconsolably.

"Why wasn't I here?" he asked himself aloud. He had already learned that Jan had died of a broken neck. Had she been conscious, her eyes searching the frightened faces working over her, hoping somehow to see him among them?

"The paramedics said she appeared unconscious," said Jim. "She didn't suffer."

From somewhere within, Terry remembered the words of English poet Thomas Carlyle, whose wife had died suddenly while he was far from home. Ironically, he had used them recently in a sermon: *"Oh, that I had you yet but for five minutes beside me, to tell you all."*

Terry looked again at his bloodstained fingers, overcome with remorse.

Why was I away from her so often? Couldn't I have helped her more with the kids? Why didn't I send flowers more often? Did I remember to say I love you the other day when we last spoke?

"Oh, that I had you by my side...."

Still kneeling in the grass, his face buried in his hands, Terry's mind flooded with more questions.

What did I do wrong to bring this on my family? God, how did I let you down? Why didn't you protect them, if I was truly doing your will?

Half blind with grief, Terry stood and walked back to the car.

The next morning, at Jan's memorial service, Living Sound sang her favorite solo, *He Giveth More Grace*, and Oral Roberts gave a warm, uplifting eulogy. He spoke about Jan's lively, captivating eyes, and the pure love for God that shone through her when she sang.

More tributes followed, until it was time for Terry to speak.

How can I possibly do this? he thought, as he rose from the pew and walked up four steps to stand at the microphone. Yet with each step, he felt his strength building... only to increase even more as he began to speak.

"Even before we married, Jan struggled to accept my calling of ministering around the world and what it might cost," Terry said. "But I had a dream, I told her, and eventually it became her dream too—that one day I would stand before God and hear him say to me, 'Well done, my good and faithful servant.'

"And now she's done it. She's with Jesus, and I'm jealous that she's already seen his smile and heard those words, 'Well done.'"

But the supernatural strength that Terry experienced for those few minutes faded before he even reached his seat again.

And later at home, after everyone had offered their condolences and left, and his mom Anne had put Misty, Scotty and Becca to bed, Terry finally went to his bedroom to be alone.

Once again, the questions came. Did he ever really have a dream? Or was the whole thing a delusion?

Lord, he thought, lying back on the bed, *I wanted to dream big dreams and do big things for you. But beneath it all, the one thing I really wanted in life was to hear you say, "Well done, Terry. You gave it all you had."*

Lying there, Terry looked at his life, scattered on the floor in shreds. All the evidence was in: First, Viktor's imprisonment, then the financial catastrophe. Surely, Jan's death was the ultimate proof. If God rewarded faithfulness and obedience with blessing… then clearly he had missed the mark by light years. He'd seen Christianity that way since boyhood, trying to measure up to his own father and to the strict standards and dictates of his church. Now the sentence seemed final: His all hadn't been enough and never would be. Something about him was just defective. Maybe all his ministry dreams were just a fantasy.

The months following Jan's death were a numbing gray streak. Terry wasn't really alive anymore, but he went through the motions anyway to keep the ministry afloat, while Anne cooked, got the children up and off to school, and fitted together the pieces of an ordinary routine. When Don Moen hinted about remarriage one afternoon, Terry bristled.

"Don, I can't even *think* about getting married again for at least a couple of years," he said. Being widowed just wasn't the same as just being single.

Gradually, Terry learned to manage days at the office, although it felt empty with most of the staff laid off, since the ministry was still foundering. Nights were pure agony. After Anne had put the children to bed and gone to her room, he'd get in his car and drive the back roads of south Tulsa, or find an all-night coffee shop just to be near people.

Even Viktor's prison would be better, he told himself over an empty cup one miserable night. *Or death. But not this living hell of guilt and grief and loneliness.*

For a month, Terry considered quitting the ministry, but something in him just wouldn't allow it. He thought of Oral and Evelyn Roberts. Over the past few years they had experienced the triple tragedy of losing their daughter and son-in-law in a plane crash, and then their oldest son. Yet somehow Oral had found the strength to go on telling people that "God is a good God."

How can I possibly keep going? Terry wondered. But he was desperate. He needed a lifeline, and fast. Maybe Oral could help in some way. Otherwise, he might as well just fold up the ministry for good.

The next day, in Roberts' office, all of Terry's anguish spilled out. "I'm at the end of the road. I feel like there's no life left in me."

"I'm going to tell you something that will save your life—*if* you'll do what I say," Oral advised.

Terry sat at attention, ready for anything.

"Go home," said Oral. "Get on your knees, and begin to praise the Lord."

Terry's heart sank.

That was *it*? Go home and praise the Lord? *For what?* he thought. *That my children cry themselves to sleep at night without their mother?*

"I'm sorry, Oral, but it just doesn't make any sense to praise God right now," he responded.

"You don't have to praise God *for* everything," Roberts explained. "But you can obey the Bible and praise him *in* everything, whether it's sickness or financial loss, or even the death of someone who means more to you than life itself."

As the two men continued talking, Terry heard himself raising every objection he had tried to quell in his children. Still discouraged, he finally thanked Oral and excused himself.

As Terry drove home, the trees outside looked as gray as the road, the buildings flat and lifeless. He pulled into the driveway and shut off the engine. If praise was his only way out, he was finished.

But what if...? Oral's been through it. He knows. What if there's one last chance?

That night Terry set his alarm for 5:30 a.m. and crawled into bed. It was a mercy, when he finally fell asleep. The next morning, before dawn, he crawled out of bed and forced himself to his knees.

What now?

Mechanically, he said, "Thank you, God. Praise the Lord. Hallelujah."

Immediately, a voice fired at him. *Law, you're a hypocrite. Why are you praising God? Your wife is dead. You can't mean those words. How can you praise God, feeling as bad as you do?*

For some minutes, as the light of dawn crept into his room, Terry's mind scalded him with accusations. He had to get off his knees. This was ridiculous.

He had started to get up, when the words of David came to him, words he'd scratched on a notepad during one of his bleakest moments months earlier: *I will bless the Lord at all times. His praise shall continually be in my mouth.*

He paused. *You've got to be happy to praise God, Terry. You're not good enough for God to use you. You're not good enough to be saved...*

In that moment, he saw the lie—an old one he'd stumbled over so much of his life.

Of course, I'm not "good enough." That's not the point. Yes, I'm hurting, but like Oral said, God isn't the dealer of death. He's the bringer of joy. God, you are joy.

Terry opened his eyes and stared at nothing across the room. *Maybe the grace that saved you as a teenager can save you again, Terry Law.* Setting his jaw, he closed his eyes. *I will praise you, God! I'll praise you just for who you are!*

"Bless your name, Lord!"

Nothing happened. "God, you're mighty." Pain and death and evil were laughing in his face. Sunlight grew, brushing the walls. He stayed on his knees for an hour; two hours; the words were wooden. He felt a pressure building inside.

Give it up, Terry...

He fought back. *Thank you, God. You are holy and loving. No matter what, you are worthy. Worthy!*

All at once, the pressure let loose. His hands went up, and he shouted.

"You are worthy, Lord. Praise you, Father!"

As he praised, Terry felt joy flooding in. It was as if he could see himself the way God saw him—from above. He saw anger, bitterness, self-pity. He saw the wrong thinking that had crippled him from his childhood—the idea that God loved him and used him only when he did good things, but was ready to cast him away when he displeased him.

"Forgive me for accusing you, Father," he prayed.

For hours, Terry prayed, walking about the room with hands held high, kneeling in adoration. Cleansing came. Healing. When he rose from his knees for the last time, a little past ten that morning, he knew a miracle had taken place.

He didn't understand it. But at a deep level, he knew.

For the next several weeks, Terry searched the Bible as if he had just discovered it. Thanksgiving and praise were everywhere in the scriptures. Why hadn't he seen it before? Hadn't he quoted the words of Jonah that first awful day on the plane?

But I, with a song of thanksgiving, with sacrifice to you.

Everywhere he looked, in the *Old Testament* Psalms, in the *New Testament* Book of Hebrews, there it was: a sacrifice of thanksgiving and praise. Even when they had been beaten and thrown in jail in the Book of Acts, "at midnight Paul and Silas prayed and sang praises to God."

That verse had always bothered Terry in the past, but now he could see: The apostles were praising the goodness of God. And it was that sacrifice of praise that had triggered the earthquake that caused the doors of their prison to fling open, paving the way to their freedom.

Wasn't that what had happened to him? Hadn't he been locked in a prison of grief, and bound for most of his life by the chains of a "you're not good enough" legalism? But just as in the Book of Acts, a sacrifice of praise had set him free.

Terry picked up the phone. "Go through every arrangement in Living Sound's repertoire," he told Don Moen. "Throw out anything that's not specifically about praise and worship. From now on, we're not singing anything else!"

Terry's preaching, and the ministry of Living Sound itself, were transformed. For the next two years, he and Don conducted praise and worship crusades across the USA, while the teams carried their new mandate around the world. Soon, he was receiving invitations to speak and write in a host of forums both old and new. By 1985, he had compiled a mountain of research into book form, and within months *The Power of Praise and Worship* had become the definitive book on the subject, with its first edition reaching nearly 200,000 sales.

With a new worship movement already springing up all over the nation, Terry's office was besieged with requests. Could he speak for this conference, write for that magazine, or appear on someone's TV show? A series of worship-themed articles he wrote for a magazine called *New Wine* received such an overwhelming response that its parent company, *Integrity Communications*, started a new recording label, *Hosanna! Music*, dedicated exclusively to recording and distributing the latest worship songs from around the world. And just as with Terry's book, their sales exploded out of the gate.

"It's like God's given you a Midas Touch," a friend said. "Everything you touch turns to gold. Several pastors have even taken to calling you 'the apostle of praise and worship.'"

"That's a bit extreme," replied Terry. "But at least they're calling."

And they were. For now, at least, pastors were calling.

CHAPTER 11

AFTERMATH

THE LATE 1980s BROUGHT a whirlwind of change across the world, especially in Eastern Europe, and Terry knew that his ministry, too, would have to change to keep up. For one thing, *Hosanna! Music* had featured Don Moen on one of their first albums, and when it became clear that *Give Thanks* was going to "go gold," Hosanna asked Don to consider joining them full-time as an artist and producer.

"Terry, what should I do?" asked Don. "You and I have worked together for a long time, but something inside me says this is the right move."

"Go ahead, Don," advised Terry. "I think God is moving you into a great new chapter in your life. And it's time to take Living Sound off the road anyway. There are so many other groups traveling now that our teams can't even pay for themselves, much less support the work overseas. I think we can find a way to minister more efficiently."

Giving Don his blessing to leave the ministry was hard, but Terry knew better than to fall into the comfort trap Oral Roberts had warned him about years earlier. If God really was in Don's departure, he reasoned, then something new and fantastic must be on the way.

And it was.

Little more than a year after Don's move to Alabama, *Hosanna! Music* had supplied Terry with a Russian version of *Give Thanks*. By 1989, he was using Jon Karner's tape duplicators, still successfully hidden from the Soviet authorities, to distribute nearly half a million albums on cassette from one end of the USSR to the other.

It felt as if the whole world was shifting and an era was changing. What lay ahead? Terry couldn't see the road, but something inside told him that unimaginably big doors were about to open. He even went so far as to predict the collapse of the Soviet Union before a conference crowd of 5,000 pastors in Tulsa.

Then in 1991, the floodgates opened, when the USSR did indeed fall completely apart. This time Terry was ready, and just as in Poland fifteen years earlier, he found himself in a perfect storm of opportunity. By the end of the year he had renamed his ministry *World Compassion*, and was delivering medicine and medical equipment to victims of the Chernobyl nuclear disaster, tons of food to starving Russian pensioners, and millions of Bibles all over the *former* Soviet Union. At one point, he even appeared on Russia's primetime newscast, *Good Evening, Moscow*, where the news anchor gave him several minutes to answer the question: "What does this Bible say?"

Like Don Moen's record career, Terry's ministry had gone gold. And yet behind the scenes, his second marriage was in shambles.

"I don't have any idea how to explain this publicly," he told Jim Gilbert one day over a late breakfast at the Dallas airport in late summer 1998. Jim had moved to Florida, and the two didn't see each other very often anymore, but today their layovers at DFW had coincided long enough for them to catch a quick meal in the terminal.

"I feel like such a fool," said Terry after the two men had placed their orders. "Fourteen million *Guideposts Magazine* subscribers read about our fairytale romance, but the truth is our marriage was a sham from the start."

As Terry unfolded his knife and fork from his napkin, a tear forced its way down his cheek, bringing a shocked look to Jim's face. With the exception of Jan's death sixteen years earlier, Terry had never been the crying type. Now, three agonizing years in divorce court had put his emotions on lockdown.

"Terry, your integrity speaks for itself," reassured Jim. "Every one of us who's seen your second marriage up close knows it was difficult, and we know you did your best."

"No, I didn't," said Terry, staring down at his plate. "For one thing, I've failed all six of my children, because I was afraid to face the truth for their sakes. Sure, I can say I was trying to protect my family or that I did everything I could to make it work. But when you get right down to it I should have been more discerning from the start. It's my fault—this whole disaster is my fault."

Terry sat silently for a moment, poking at egg whites with his fork, feeling miserable. Then he lifted his head to speak again.

"You know what's even worse? *Guideposts* has decided to reprint the story. I called and told them we're in the midst of a divorce, but they're going to do it anyway. This huge lie is still spreading, and I can't stop it."

"Terry, God brought you through Jan's death," said Jim, "and he'll bring you through this, too."

"Maybe, but divorce does even more damage than death," said Terry. "I didn't think there could be anything more horrible than losing Jan, but when it happened at least the kids and I could deal with the finality of it. But divorce? It's like a big wreck where the cars just keep crashing into one another, and the victims' injuries keep getting worse."

Terry lowered his eyes again, and thought of his six children.

"There are so many victims in this."

The two men ate quickly, and then it was time to go. Terry picked up the tab and then waited while Jim boarded the transfer train at Terminal D. He'd have to run to make his own connection, but it was okay. Old friends had become more important than ever, now that he felt so alone.

After rushing to his gate and onto the plane, Terry hoisted his carry-on bag into the bin over his seat in First Class. It had felt good to get things off his chest back there, and now his complimentary upgrade was turning the weekend travel grind into a good Saturday. He hoped tomorrow would go well, too, and it probably would, unless his hosts said something like "Flying home to the wife?"—then it could turn bad quickly.

The plane departed on time and soon the Dallas suburbs had faded beneath a layer of clouds. Terry watched the white puffs recede beneath his window, while his mind rewound 13 years into the past, to the early days of his failed marriage.

Back in 1985, Terry's storybook romance with a beautiful young widow had taken his rapidly growing audience by storm. And after *The Power of Praise and Worship* had become a hot seller, a his-and-her sequel had also done well, especially after the original *Guideposts* article had set the stage.

Why didn't I just refuse the interviews and admit the trouble we were having, right then? he asked himself yet again. *Why did I think sheer willpower could fix it?*

Terry thought back to the end of those first eighteen months, right after Laurie's birth, when his supposed "miraculous marriage" had gone from bad to worse.

"I couldn't figure it out," he had told Jim. "I kept thinking it must be faults of mine that Jan had overlooked, or that I was too focused on projects and lacked sensitivity—I'd heard that from Living Sound teams. All I knew was that I wanted to get things right, but nothing seemed to work."

He had done his best, Terry told himself. But as he stared at the blanket of clouds below, a question surfaced. He had tried hard, yes, but at some point had his faith and persistence simply become an exercise in denial?

Lord, you know I wasn't faking anything. I loved her. There's no way in the world I would've ever filed for divorce.

Terry closed his eyes and thought back to his Canadian Pentecostal upbringing. Divorce was *never* an option and *always* a sin—his dad had emphasized that. "Every marriage can be healed, Terry, and if it fails there are no innocent parties."

Even as a rebellious teenager, raging at the idea he could never be good enough for God *or* his father, Terry had vowed that this was one area of his life where his parents would see him succeed. He would never, *ever* get a divorce, no matter what. Other people's marriages might fall apart, but not his. Reading Kenneth Hagin's faith teaching after his conversion, and then working closely with Oral Roberts, had only reinforced his determination to succeed. And as far as the ministry was concerned, he had the track record to prove it. For the past 13 years, even in his lowest moments, God had blessed that area of his life.

But here he was, not only going through a divorce, but one that had dragged out so long that now he just wanted it to be over. Three years of an opposing lawyer's endless attacks on his character had drained him. A final decree would at least bring some measure of relief. But it would also mean admitting that in the singularly most important area of his life, he had failed. And not just himself, but his children, his ministry...and God.

Terry shifted in his seat and tried to clear his thoughts. He needed to put his mind on idle for a while, and started to reach for the inflight magazine, before noticing that the flight attendant was serving a meal. He chose filet mignon over chicken, and was suddenly glad to have ignored his bacon and eggs back in Dallas. Steak would stay with him longer, a good thing since he'd be arriving in New York too late to have dinner with his host pastor.

I wonder if he'll ask me "the question" when I see him tomorrow morning, thought Terry. *What will I say if he asks me "How's your wife?"*

He had deflected the question the first few times people asked it. "Back in Tulsa, probably out shopping somewhere," he had said, as if the joke might defuse their curiosity. But it didn't always work, and once he had actually breached the truth and said, "She's fine. We're doing great."

Now he faced the real reason why: If you were in ministry, divorce was unpardonable. Period.

"I know lying's wrong," he had told Larry Dalton, another old friend whose fellowship he prized like rediscovered treasure. "But it would be so awkward to just blurt out the truth. And there would be consequences. I'd become a marked man, and it wouldn't matter who's at fault. Divorce is a 'scarlet letter.' You know, when you're widowed everybody rushes to your side, but when you're divorced they scatter. It's like you've got the plague."

Terry's plane landed in upstate New York that evening, and

after settling into his hotel he decided to watch television until he fell asleep. It really didn't matter what was on, as long as it helped keep him from lying there all night, rehashing the last few hours on the plane.

He was on autopilot the next morning, but both services went well, and afterward, Terry climbed into his rental car to follow the pastor and his wife to the restaurant. Telling the congregation how a highly placed Chinese official had secretly given him more than a million confiscated Bibles to distribute had been a home run, and he knew this pastor was a friend and supporter in the making. Now there would be lunch and conversation for an hour or two, and then he would head back to the airport to catch his flight home to Tulsa. Then, tomorrow morning, he'd be back in court.

The two cars parked in front of the steakhouse and Terry walked with his hosts to their table, where another couple had gone ahead to shorten the wait. Terry shook their hands and thanked them as he took a seat. A pot of coffee and a basket of warm rolls were already waiting by his plate.

The five had not been chatting for more than a couple of minutes when the pastor's wife took a sip of water and dabbed her lipstick before turning her full attention to Terry. The real conversational kick-off was on its way.

"Tell me, how does your wife handle all the traveling you do around the world, especially in so many danger zones?" she asked.

Terry froze.

I knew it, he thought, as the heat began to creep up from his collar. *I knew on the plane yesterday this was going to happen. Oh God, what now?*

Terry realized that everyone at the table could see his face turning red, like it always did when he was flustered. Regardless of what he would say, it was already obvious that this woman had hit a nerve.

"My...wife filed for divorce three years ago," said Terry in a subdued, matter-of-fact voice. "I...."

He started to continue, but nothing more came out. What was the use? Nothing he could say was going to save this poor pastor's wife from the mortified look that had just frozen her face. And nothing was going to change the expression of sudden regret that her husband wore.

Terry had seen that look before. It said: *I wish we could just roll back the calendar and cancel these meetings, so they never happened.*

Never mind that God had blessed his ministry to the church that morning, or the work in China, or the fact that so many mouths were being fed and lives changed. Never mind that a divorce involving an evangelist was not automatically the evangelist's fault.

Never mind the truth.

"I don't care who's to blame—I don't want a divorced person in my pulpit." That was what one pastor had told Joel when he had called to cancel at the last minute. And that summed it up. That same sentence was written across *this* pastor's face, right this very minute.

As he flew home that afternoon, Terry quit the ministry for at least the hundredth time in the past three years. Why not just get in his car at the Tulsa airport and head for Florida or somewhere up in the mountains? Why not lose himself somewhere far away, where nobody would ever recognize him and start asking insulting questions? If it weren't for his three children still living at home, he might do it.

A dark sky covered downtown Tulsa the next morning as Terry

made his way to court. No storm had been forecast, but this was Oklahoma, after all, where TV weathermen spent half of their airtime explaining why they had gotten it wrong the day before.

How fitting, thought Terry, as he searched for covered parking in case there was hail. You never knew what to expect from a surprise storm.

If this doesn't describe my life, nothing does, he told himself, as he wondered whether the climate inside the court would match the one out here. The opposing lawyer was always filing some new motion, no matter how absurd, to try and get his hands on the ministry's assets. But at least the first judge had dismissed them all, and he hoped that this new one who had just taken over would do the same.

"Listen, Terry," his lawyer, Bob Bartz, whispered after his Honor had sounded the gavel to start the day's proceedings. "That other attorney is well aware that the private disposition of a non-profit ministry's assets is illegal in every state of the union, and he's hoping the new judge doesn't know. He's wasting time and his client's money, but we've just got to let it play itself out."

"I guess you're right," replied Terry, "but it's not easy, Bob. Last week, he made me feel like scum so badly that I felt like I needed to go home and take a shower."

As soon as Terry had whispered those words, an idea hit him. He reached for a fresh legal pad and began to write.

Isaiah 54:17

"No weapon formed against you shall prosper, and every tongue which rises against you in judgment you shall condemn. This is the heritage of the servants of the Lord, and their righteousness is from Me," says the Lord.

Terry put down his pen and looked at the words he had just written. Why hadn't he thought of this before? Way back in Medicine Hat, when he had spent a week praying and fasting in a friend's living room, he had memorized important Bible verses by writing them out, and then rehearsing them out loud until he knew them by heart. And sixteen years ago, after Jan had died and Oral Roberts had told him to start praising God, he had filled page after page with verses on praise.

Terry looked again at the verse from Isaiah. He couldn't recite the words aloud here in court, but he could sure block out the insults being hurled at him by repeating them in his mind.

Terry looked at his attorney and saw him grin as he read the words on the pad. *Thumbs up*, he signaled, with a wink of approval.

This is the key, Lord, thought Terry. *This is how I'm going to make it. I'm going to sit here and offer a sacrifice of praise no matter how long this hell lasts.*

* * *

The months flew by after that, as Terry filled one yellow pad after another with words of praise to God. At last, in mid-July 1999, nearly four years after he had walked into this very courtroom, Terry stood to shake his attorney's hand. It was finally over. There was nothing more to do now, said Bob, than wait for the judge's decree and terms of settlement.

"I've got to go to Wales for some ministry," replied Terry, "but I'll make sure there's always a fax machine around, so you can let me know the minute it's over."

"I'll be on call around the clock," said Bob. "In the meantime, let's just praise God that this part is finished."

"Well, let's hope my ministry's not finished, too," smiled Terry—only half joking.

The two men shook hands a final time, and Terry picked up his briefcase to leave.

"Excuse me, Dr. Law?"

Terry turned and was surprised to see the court stenographer standing before him. For the past two years, this woman had sat in the courtroom, recording every word spoken. Just as he had written volumes of Bible verses by hand, she had written every accusation, every insult that had been hurled his way.

"Excuse me, Dr. Law, but I was wondering...." She looked a bit tentative, and Terry wondered what on earth an officer of the court might have to say to him.

"The other stenographers and a couple of the bailiffs and I get together every week for a Bible study. We were wondering if you might be available to come and speak to us sometime soon."

Terry was stunned, and could feel himself turning red. But for the first time in ages it actually felt good to blush.

"I'd be delighted!" he said, trying to sound cordial and not give away the giddy feeling rising inside him. "I'd be happy to come very soon. Thank you, Ma'am. Thank you. This means so much."

After taking his leave, Terry nearly floated back to the parking garage. The sky outside was hazy today, but it no longer reflected the state of his life. He climbed into his car and turned the key, his mind returning once again to Isaiah 54:17, the verse of scripture he had written by hand at the start of every court appearance for the past eight or nine months.

"Every tongue which rises against you in judgment you shall condemn. This is the heritage of the servants of the Lord, and their

righteousness is from Me."

You said it, God. You said it!

* * *

Terry had ministered across Wales for more than a week, and was about to crawl under the covers at his hotel in Newport when there was a knock on his door. He looked at the red numbers on the clock. Nearly midnight. He walked over and looked through the peephole.

Another knock. "Fax for you, sir," said a man's voice.

Terry opened the door and the desk clerk handed him a large, thick envelope, before politely excusing himself and walking back down the hall.

Feels like a lot of pages, thought Terry, bouncing the envelope up and down in his hand a couple of times. *Maybe I'd better go for a walk, in case there's something in here I need to call Bob about.*

Terry pulled on his shirt and jeans and quickly made his way downstairs and through the lobby's rear exit, into the courtyard.

His hands trembled slightly as he removed the contents of the envelope and quickly scanned past the legalese at the top of the page. He had to find the phrase that could mark the beginning of major changes his life: *In the matter of such and such this court finds in favor of...*

He searched with his finger until he found the section that dealt with the accusations against him.

...this court finds in favor of the defendant...the defendant...the defendant....

Terry tried to slow himself as he flipped through the pages, but his racing heart refused. He could hardly believe his eyes. Every argument, every ugly accusation against him, had been pronounced "without merit."

"Thank you, Father!" he yelled into the night air. "Thank you, Jesus. Praise your name!"

Bedroom lights were flipping on in the floors above him, but Terry didn't care. For the first time in as long as he could remember, he *did—not—care!*

You're 56 years old without a nickel to your name, he told himself. *But at least you've got six children who love you, and you've got your name. More than that you've got the name of Jesus.*

A Bible verse he had written dozens of times on his legal pad leapt to mind. Hebrews 13:15 had been one of his first big "praise and worship" discoveries sixteen years earlier. Now he felt like quoting it again, and if he woke anybody up—well, they needed to hear it, too.

"*Therefore by Him let us continually offer the sacrifice of praise to God*," he said in his best preaching voice, "*that is, the fruit of our lips, giving thanks to His name.*"

As soon as he had quoted the verse, Terry realized just how tired he felt. Not worn out or fatigued, like he'd felt for countless years, but a satisfied kind of tired, like a Super Bowl winner must feel in an empty locker room, after the last reporter has gone home.

True, he had no trophy, and even though he had been vindicated, Terry was dead broke, had lost several old friends and his reputation in many churches had been shattered. Yet in the oddest way, he felt richer and freer now. Like St. Paul, he was satisfied to know beyond all doubt that God was faithful, and to "owe no one anything, except to love each other."

Get some sleep, Terry, said something inside him—only it was more of a feeling than a voice. *Sleep long and hard, and get back home to your children. You've got great things coming. "Eye hasn't seen and ear hasn't heard" things.*

Such a wonderful but wordless sense of wellbeing could hardly have struck Terry as a prophecy that night in 1999. After all, there were no audible voices or tremors rushing through him as they had in the defining moments of his past. Instead, as he sank into bed and drifted into his first good night of sleep in more than a decade, a tiny spark rekindled something in his spirit. It was the same something that had made him dance in the rain and chase lightning when he was five. It was the thing that had gone wrong in him in his teens when he built a bomb, and then gone right when he had faced down the Russian KGB. It was his sense of adventure, his love of the storm.

The Storm Chaser was back, proven, primed and ready. And just in time, because in less than two years, the whole world was indeed going to change.

CHAPTER 12

STORM OF
THE CENTURY

WHILE JOEL PAID THE TAXI DRIVER, Terry stood with his suitcase at his side and surveyed the scene before him, knowing he was called to be here—and also wondering if one of these missions was going be his last. Given the scene unfolding before him, his question wasn't far-fetched.

The Pakistani Army's *al Khalid* tanks flanking the entrance of the Quetta Serena Hotel were big, but not nearly as imposing as he had expected...or hoped. The hotel looked small too, and vulnerable, considering the scars of war that pitted its facade. But it was the safest place in town—Voice of America and CNN were broadcasting war coverage from the roof every night—so he was glad to call it home.

"I think this is the first time I've ever seen battle-ready tanks and camels on the same day," said Terry, as he and Joel unfolded their passports for the sentry, and then made their way to the check-in desk. The Serena's warm lobby was a very welcome change from the icy November air outside, which was pouring down through the Toba Kakar Mountains surrounding this mile-high city just east of the border with Afghanistan.

"Interesting place, for sure," said Joel forcing a smile. Over the years, pleasantness had become a reflex for him. But there was no denying the tension they both felt, knowing they had just flown into a war zone and a city on high-alert.

"Why not just go to your room and unwind?" suggested Terry, handing Joel his key. "I'll call you later."

Terry entered his own room and locked the door behind him, then hoisted his well-worn Hartmann suitcase onto the spare bed that lay nearer the window.

What can I possibly accomplish in such an impossible situation, Lord? he prayed as he unzipped the lid and began unpacking. It was the same question he had asked God a hundred times back in his own living room over the past seven weeks since September 11, the day that had changed the world.

* * *

Terry had been in a Tulsa hospital bed that morning, recovering from minor surgery, when his cell phone rang.

"Terry, turn on the TV right now." Jim's voice was forceful. "Don't ask questions. Just do it."

The hands on the clock in Terry's Tulsa room had read 8:07 when he clicked the power button on his bedside remote. And then before his eyes, the world had changed. Both towers of New York City's World Trade Center were on fire, huge charcoal clouds billowing so heavily from their upper floors that they looked more like the giant smoke stacks of an oil refinery than the famed icons of American commerce.

In the short terrible time it took the towers to collapse, a question formed in Terry's mind—one that had eventually brought him here to Pakistan.

What can I do, Lord? What does one man have to offer in a world suddenly thrown into such turmoil?

For a month and a half, Terry had watched a war unfold. President George Bush had blamed a terrorist named Osama bin Laden for the attacks that killed nearly 3,000 Americans on 9/11, and had unleashed an air and ground assault on Afghanistan in an effort to bring him to justice, and to overthrow the Taliban regime that had given him safe haven.

At first, Terry had felt sheer anger at the attacks, like everyone else who had a soul. But as the weeks dragged on, the news showed fewer terrorists being captured, and more and more civilians fleeing for their lives. Day after day, thousands of Afghan families from cities like Kabul and Kandahar were streaming on foot across the high desert into western Pakistan. Before long, Terry's intense anger at the terrorists had tangled with his growing compassion for the refugees, resulting in a level of frustration and helplessness he had never known.

The two years since Terry's divorce had gradually reinvigorated him. Yes, some pastors had severed ties with him, just as he had expected. But others had rallied to his side, and with the expansion of World Compassion's missions in China, Tibet and Nepal, new churches were coming on board. His ministry had been progressing at a faster clip than ever, especially since he had discovered the unexpected freedom that came with losing everything. It was as though all the hollowing out by death and divorce had left him with a greater capacity to serve God.

As a result, Terry had been taking bigger risks than ever, assisting underground churches in forbidden zones like Laos, Burma and Nepal, and sneaking rice and Bibles across a frozen river into famine-ravaged North Korea. The truth was, as a single man now, he really didn't care whether he lived or died.

Terry had never told a soul, but the idea of dying for the cause of Christ inwardly elevated him. No, he hadn't gone to prison like his friend, Viktor, but he had certainly had the life wrenched out of him in other ways. More than once, Viktor's words had echoed within him as though they were his own: "I died the day I gave my life to Jesus. They can't kill me again."

Somehow, the single life had given him singular purpose. He was always ready to act, to die, to do anything but sit still, which was exactly how he had spent the past seven weeks...until the previous Friday.

"God, they're such savages," he had growled that morning in his living room. "The Taliban kill their own people in the name of Allah." The agony of doing nothing had become unbearable, and Terry had nearly thrown a book at the TV. But what *could* he do? In the face of such unprecedented tragedy, World Compassion seemed small, and Terry felt smaller still. He felt agitated.

Realizing that fact had brought the answer, though: *Get control of your anger and agitation. Be still. Listen.* And at last, the inner voice he had waited for weeks to hear spoke clearly.

So what will you do? Are you going to sit here cursing the darkness, or will you go and light a candle?

The question was still lingering in Terry's mind when a loud boom from the desert shook the walls of his hotel room in Quetta, snapping him back to the present. Grabbing his room key, he rushed out the door and headed for the lobby. He needed to find a man named Peter Kessler, the U.N. High Commissioner for Refugees. For all practical purposes Kessler was the current king of Quetta, and the man who would tell Terry how to find the *Killi Faizo* refugee camp he had read about in last week's *TIME*.

Terry searched the hotel's corridors until at last he spotted a small laminate plaque bearing the letters UNHCR on a door that was ajar. Within moments he was shaking hands and introducing himself to the Commissioner, who wore a look of complete surprise.

"Why in the world are you here, Dr. Law?" asked Kessler. He looked young for a high-ranking U.N. official.

"I operate a relief ministry headquartered in Oklahoma," said Terry. "My assistant and I are here to help with the situation at *Killi Faizo.*"

Kessler frowned and wagged his head. "Sorry. Not possible. As soon as those people find out you're Americans, you'll be killed. And besides that, this hotel just went on lockdown for a week, so you can't leave. Frankly, I don't know how you managed to make it here in the first place."

"Sir, I'm aware of the danger," protested Terry, "but we've got a lot of experience, and are prepared for whatever happens. We know we're on our own."

"Sorry. Final word," replied Kessler, turning aside to resume reading the stack of bulletins he had laid on his desk when Terry entered.

"Thank you, sir," said Terry.

Kessler didn't look up.

Got to get to Joel's room and make a plan, thought Terry, striding down the hall to the elevator. *If God told me to come here, he's going to unlock a door no U.N. commissioner can lock.*

The elevator door opened on 3, and Terry searched the hall until he found Joel's room. He was starting to knock, when a vague memory stirred in his mind.

"Joel, doesn't World Compassion have a partner back in Tulsa whose brother lives in Pakistan?" asked Terry, as soon as the door opened.

"Yes, we do," said Joel. "Dr. Catherine Earls has an adopted brother who is a missionary here somewhere. I think he might have been born in this country."

To Terry's delight he had a strong signal on his cell phone, and within a couple of minutes he heard the voice of his doctor friend back in Tulsa.

"Dr. Earls, I'm in Pakistan, and in a bit of a hurry," explained Terry. "If I remember right, you've a got a brother living somewhere over here, and I'd like to try and contact him. Do you have his number?"

"Oh yes, Terry," replied the doctor. "My brother David lives in western Pakistan, in Quetta, near the border with Afghanistan."

Terry was nearly dancing when he dialed David's local number from the hotel phone, and within an hour the dark, handsome missionary had joined him in Joel's room.

"I pastor a church very near to here," said David, "and *Killi Faizo* is only a few kilometers away. I can take you."

Just like that, the impossible had become possible. Once again, Terry had found his way to the eye of the storm.

* * *

Getting out of lockdown the next day after lunch proved easier than Terry had expected, thanks to David's persuasive ways with one of the sentries. Forty-five minutes later, the three men had passed through the border town of Chaman, and into camp *Killi Faizo*.

David eased his SUV past a group of children playing kickball in the dirt with what looked like an old doll's head, then drove another 100 yards past dozens of makeshift lean-tos, before stopping in front of a sturdy looking tent straight ahead.

"Come with me," said David, as he opened the driver's door and walked toward the tent. "I'll introduce you to the camp commander."

A moment later, Terry and Joel were met by a Pakistani officer dressed in fatigues. They each shook his hand as David introduced them, and then Terry came to the point, explaining why he and Joel had come to *Killi Faizo*.

"We'd like to find out what the people's most urgent needs are," said Terry. "We're not sure how much we can do, but we're here to help."

The commander waggled his head from side-to-side in approval. He looked surprised but pleased.

"Come inside," he said, with a hint of eagerness. "I will explain."

The commander led the three men into his tent, past a folding table strewn with papers, to a large tote board covered with writing and statistics.

"There are nine thousand Afghans here," he said, pointing to the board, "and we are already nearing maximum capacity. As it is, we lack even basic supplies, so anything you can provide will be greatly appreciated by these people."

Terry looked at the board, which was arranged in various columns, written in the Pashto alphabet. It looked like scribbles to his western eyes, but at least there were numbers to the left and right of each notation.

"The columns show the food and supplies we have on-hand," the commander said, pointing to a stack of numbers on the right. "The larger number to the left of each item represents what we lack."

Terry looked at the totals. The column on the left added up

to a much larger sum than the one on the right. Then he noticed a set of hash marks written near the right edge of the board. The area was smudged, and looked as though it had been erased and corrected many times. The marks were arranged in groups of five—four vertical lines with a fifth slashed diagonally—the kind a school teacher might draw for children learning to count.

"What do these marks represent?" asked Terry, touching his index finger to that part of the board.

"They indicate the number of children who freeze to death each night. The desert temperatures drop precipitously after sunset, and most people do not have blankets. Even with their parents holding them, the smaller children often do not survive. We lose an average of twelve per night."

A chill shot up Terry's spine. He steadied himself, and struggled to stay composed.

"How is this possible?" he asked in a trembling voice. "Quetta is only 20 miles away, and we passed a busy market in the city center when we left there this afternoon."

"Yes," replied the commander with a shrug. "But the people of Quetta do not consider the needs of Afghans to be a matter for their concern."

Terry stared at the marks without speaking, his mind numbed by the shock that they each represented a tiny, lifeless body.

One candle, Terry. You can light at least one candle in this darkness, said the voice in his spirit. *That's why I brought you here.*

"Please take this, sir," said Terry, pulling off his jacket and handing it to the commander. Beside him, Joel and David were removing their coats, as well.

"Give our coats to whomever needs them most. We don't have time to gather supplies before tonight, but we'll return tomorrow with as much as we can find."

Terry shook hands with the commander and thanked him, before turning to speak to Joel and David.

"Come on," he said. "Let's get back to Quetta and rent some trucks. We're going to buy everything we can get our hands on."

The air flooding down from the mountains was blistering cold the next morning when David arrived at the Serena, six ramshackle trucks trailing closely behind his SUV. At the sight of the trucks, the hatches on the tanks clanked shut, and every soldier standing guard raised his rifle, lowering them only when Terry and Joel climbed into the SUV and led the convoy away from the hotel.

Three hours later, Terry had cleaned out every shop in central Quetta's *Kabari Bazar,* and the trucks were stacked high, their canvas coverings holding food, medicine, and more than 5,000 blankets and coats. Driving into the camp, they looked as though they might tip over. Heeding Terry's advice, the commander had erected an extra tent and surrounded it with armed guards, where Terry and his crew could safely offload and distribute the supplies without causing a riot.

For nearly 16 hours over the next two days, Afghan men, women, and children walked into the tent to receive their gifts, often bowing in the dirt and weeping, as though the life-saving blankets had been spun from gold.

"Why are you doing this?" the commander asked Terry midway through one of the marathons, his voice quavering slightly.

"Let me show you," said Terry, reaching into his shirt pocket for the small New Testament he always carried with him.

"Look at what Jesus said in this Bible." He turned to Matthew, chapter 25 and pointed to verse 35.

"'For I was hungry and you gave Me food; I was thirsty and you gave Me drink; I was a stranger and you took Me in; I *was* naked and you clothed Me; I was sick and you visited Me; I was in prison and you came to Me.'

"Then the righteous will answer Him, saying, 'Lord, when did we see You hungry and feed You, or thirsty and give You drink? When did we see You a stranger and take You in, or naked and clothe You? Or when did we see You sick, or in prison, and come to You?' And the King will answer and say to them, 'Assuredly, I say to you, inasmuch as you did it to one of the least of these My brethren, you did it to Me.'"

"The Bible says that in serving these people we are serving Jesus himself, sir," explained Terry, raising his eyes from the page. "Their lives are precious to him, and to us. And every time we hand them a blanket, we're handing it to Jesus, as well. We came because we want these people to know that Jesus loves them, and can save their souls as well as their bodies."

Three days later, Terry snoozed in comfort aboard his long flight home, often stirring himself to relive those life-changing hours in the tent at *Killi Faizo*. Somehow, he told Joel, they had to go back.

The morning air was even colder than it had been two months earlier, when David's SUV left the Serena Hotel in January to take Terry, Joel, and Terry's son, Scot, around the mountains to the sprawling *Mohammed Khail* camp an hour south of Quetta, where 90,000 refugees were living in the dirt—ten times as many as at *Killi Faizo*. This time there were nine trucks laden with supplies, and Terry had sent them on ahead at sunrise. With so many more refugees to feed and clothe this time, his team had needed the extra hour of sleep in order to operate at peak efficiency.

"Got more candles this time," said Terry to no one in particular as he stared out the passenger window. Joel and Scot looked at one another, puzzled, while David dodged ruts in the road.

The trucks were lined up and waiting at the camp's gate when the SUV arrived, and David signaled them to move out. They hadn't gone more than a quarter-mile in when suddenly the convoy stopped. From all directions, people were running, a few at first, and then hundreds, toward the trucks.

"Stay here while David I and take a look," said Terry to his crew as he opened the passenger door.

The two men had walked forward past four or five trucks when the driver of the lead vehicle stumbled into sight, his face covered with blood. Something glittered in his beard, and suddenly Terry realized the man's head was covered with broken glass. His windshield had been shattered.

Beside him, Terry heard David let out a loud moan.

"Oh, no!" yelled David. "Look. Someone has put big signs on the sides of the trucks. They say, 'World Compassion. America,' in Pashto. They want to kill us. We've got to get out of here, now!"

Terry and David sprinted back to the SUV and jumped in quickly, while a Pakistani soldier piled in the back seat and pushed Joel to the center. The soldier looked terrified, but Terry was glad to see him and motioned for him to keep his gun visible.

"Everybody white, get down!" yelled David, as he pressed the accelerator. "Some men out there will have guns, too, and they will aim for you first."

Hundreds of men and boys were picking up stones and running toward the convoy. Even a few women were joining the fray.

"Where can we go?" yelled Terry, as a rock bounced off the SUV's front fender.

"There's a U.N. fort about two kilometers straight ahead," said David, weaving to keep from hitting a young boy with his arm in motion. "The driver up front knows to follow the tank tracks."

After a few hundred feet, the convoy had accelerated to about fifteen miles per hour, and Terry felt safe enough to raise his eyes just above the dashboard. Ahead, as far as he could see, angry Afghans were positioning themselves on either side of the track, their arms raised and their hands full of anything hard enough to throw. As the trucks passed, the arms swung down in sequence, the angry gauntlet of men hurling volley after volley of stones. Inside the SUV, the team flinched and bobbed as all around them metal crunched and windows cracked. Still crouching to hide his color, Terry searched the crowd with his eyes, hoping against hope to see only rocks and not rifles.

"We're nearly there," shouted David, as the hail of projectiles increased. "They're bunched up near the walls, so it's going to get heavy."

As the gates of the fort opened, the nine trucks sped up and fanned out to make room for their companions. Bringing up the rear, David drove straight for the middle and wheeled sharply around to face the gates.

Rocks were flying over the wall now, their arcs silhouetted against the sky. The wall itself couldn't be more than nine feet high, and soon Terry saw hands and faces appearing at the top. The raging crowd outside was coming in.

Suddenly there was a loud crash, and something large shattered the window beside the soldier.

"Grenade!" yelled Joel as a rock hit his knee, and reflexively he jumped right, pushing Scot hard against the door.

Beside him, the soldier screamed something in his own language, and fired his rifle through the broken window into the air. Ahead of the SUV, Afghan men and boys were diving back over the wall.

Instinctively, the nine trucks had formed a haphazard half circle, and Terry saw two drivers waving hard to get his attention. From the side, Pakistani soldiers stationed at the fort had rousted from their vehicles to guard the trucks.

"There!" shouted Terry. "Let's get between the trucks." The SUV's four doors flung open in unison, and everyone bolted for cover.

"What now?" said Scot, nearly unable to breathe. Terry's son had plenty of experience, having been on several dangerous missions to Asia, but now he was white as a sheet.

"I'm not sure," said Terry.

"You are going to die today," said one of the drivers, in heavily accented English.

"No, we're not!" replied Terry in a firm voice. "The Bible says we're protected by the blood of Jesus. We're redeemed and we're going to live."

Everyone stood quietly for a moment, looking at the front wall of the fort. Outside, the crowd was screaming curses in Pashto, but no one was coming over the wall. In his panic, the Pakistani soldier had saved the team's lives.

Terry turned to the fort's commander.

"Can you get us out of here?" he asked.

"No, I cannot," replied the officer. "But I have the telephone number of a platoon camped 40 kilometers from here. If you have a telephone, I could call them.

Terry wheeled around toward Scot.

"Do you have that new satellite phone in your bag?" he asked.

"Yes. It's charged, but I've never tried to use it."

"Hand it to the officer," said Terry. "Now's the time."

The officer made the call, and then informed Terry that troops were on their way. In the meantime they would have to wait.

More than four hours had passed when the yelling outside the fort suddenly gave way to the roar of truck engines, and what sounded like at least one tank. The Pakistani Army had arrived.

Quickly, two soldiers ran to the gates and lifted the long bar holding them closed. A moment later, the lead truck pulled into the fort, while the rest of the convoy spread into formation outside the gates.

The platoon leader climbed down from the truck. Looking at the piles of supplies, he sized up the situation.

"Do you want to take these with you, sir?" he asked.

"No, we brought them for the people outside," replied Terry. "They are in desperate need."

The platoon leader registered a look of shock.

"These people are trying to kill you, and you want to give them food?" he asked incredulously.

"Yes," said Terry. "If it's alright with you and the U.N. fort commander, my friend David would like to return next week and distribute everything to the people."

Terry turned to David.

"Is this okay?"

"Of course," replied David.

"Good," said Terry. "And while you're making arrangements, ask him to remove those stupid signs, so the drivers can come back and get their trucks."

The fort commander was as surprised as the platoon leader.

"We came a long way to help these people," said Terry, as David interpreted. "They've believed lies about Americans and about Christians, but that doesn't matter. They need our help."

Terry and David bade the officer farewell, and then everyone piled into the shelter of the covered truck, while Terry climbed up front.

The sun was setting as the military convoy slowly began making its way back to the main gate of *Mohammed Khail,* the truck carrying Terry's team ensconced safely in the middle. The track ahead was still lined with refugees holding stones, but they had lowered their arms and assumed the squatting position—feet flat and bottoms just off the ground—that was customary in this part of the world.

Terry looked forward through the windshield as the long line of trucks made its ten-minute journey back along the track. All along the way, angry Afghan refugees stared sullenly at the convoy, the trucks' headlights making their eyes glare as they crouched. In an odd way they reminded Terry of the lions he had seen years ago in the game park in South Africa.

Just four months earlier, Terry had sat in his living room back in Tulsa, helplessly railing against injustice as it played out on a small screen. *What can one man do?* he had asked, and God had told him to go and light a candle in the dark. He had obeyed, never dreaming that such a small flame could burn so brightly and save so many lives, even if it had nearly cost him his own.

You did it, son, said a still, small voice in Terry's spirit. *You came and lit a candle in the darkness. Don't worry if the people are still blinded by the light, because very soon they will see. And so will you.*

CHAPTER 13

ESCAPE

THE TURQUOISE SHALLOWS of the eastern Mediterranean were as still as warm bath water under the hot August sun, and were it not for the occasional wake of a speedboat rocking his air mattress, Terry might have slept his way to a sunburn on such a lazy afternoon. Breaking a sweat this way in Cyprus was a welcome change from his nerve-wracking escape from the Afghan mob that had tried to stone him seven months before in the Pakistani desert. But at least the people had gotten the food and blankets a week later when David returned, and many hearts had been turned to Jesus since then.

That harrowing experience had kicked off the most adventurous year of Terry's life, and since then he'd flown three times into the heart of darkness itself: Kabul, Afghanistan. With hindsight, he was glad that Scot's wife, Kathy, had insisted they join him on his initial trip in March.

"The Bible says we're to care for widows and orphans," Kathy had said. "And the Taliban have already widowed 40,000 women and countless more children in Kabul alone. Please let us help."

Terry remembered the misery of the Afghan women the previous November at *Killi Faizo*. They had cowered in the dirt as he and Joel handed out blankets.

"You are a man," the camp commander had explained, "so they

fear you. Afghan women are routinely beaten by their husbands, fathers and brothers, so they grow up fearing all men. This is the rule, not the exception."

At first, Terry had been tempted to hate every Afghan man he saw, but the men's own Taliban-inflicted injuries and stories of profound loss had made him pity the sheer savagery of their existence. More than once since then, the words of a dying Savior had come to mind: *Father forgive them. They know not what they do.*

Lying here under the summer sun, Terry felt pride in Scot's and Kathy's initiative. Their bravery in visiting a home that secretly housed and educated widows and their children had led to World Compassion's new plan to build seven more, where dozens of widows could learn enough English and sewing skills to provide for their children.

Terry rolled off his air mattress into the crystalline waters to wash the sweat off his body. It was time to join his trusted colleague, Ray Bevan, on the beach for lunch.

Hummus and *souvlakia* with flat bread made for a great beachside picnic, and Terry recounted a tale or two to Ray while they ate. As usual, the Welshman joked and made a pun about "getting stoned in Pakistan," but he was also quick to genuinely rejoice in God's goodness. The two swapped ministry stories for a few more minutes, before Ray changed the subject.

"Terry, did you know that as we sit here we're only 125 miles from Beirut, Lebanon?" asked Ray, pointing eastward across the sea.

"You're kidding," replied Terry. "We're that close to the Middle East?"

As the words left his lips, something leapt in Terry's heart. *The Middle East.*

Oh Lord, what now? he thought to himself. For the rest of the afternoon and into the evening, he tried to shake off the thought, but it wouldn't leave him alone. And after all these years, he knew better than to keep resisting.

It was nearly midnight in Cyprus when Terry picked up his cell phone and dialed the one Tulsa number that always answered.

"Joel," said Terry a moment later. "We're going to the Middle East."

"Ah...okay. Where in the Middle East?"

"I have no idea. I only know we're supposed to go."

"What do you want me to do next?"

"Make some calls and find the most effective ministries there. Then let's pick the most promising destinations and go. God will show us what to do when we get there."

After four months of research, Terry and Joel made a whirlwind tour through Egypt, Syria, Lebanon, and Israel, finally landing in Jordan a few days before Christmas. Having spent eight frustrating days on the move with nothing to show for it but jet lag, Terry was counting on this evening's dinner with the local United Bible Society director to prove that he hadn't been suffering sunstroke when he had heard that little voice back in Cyprus.

"I live here in Amman, but most of my work takes place in Iraq," said Nabil Omeish, as the three took their seats in the hotel restaurant. "I am Jordanian, but my wife grew up in Baghdad, Iraq."

Just as in Cyprus, when Ray had mentioned Beirut, something quickened in Terry's spirit.

"Iraq—really?" said Terry. "You and your wife must lead interesting lives. Maybe we could meet her as well while we're here."

"Oh, it's my father-in-law, General Georges Sada, whom you should really meet," said Nabil. "He is an Assyrian Christian. He works for Saddam Hussein."

"What?" Terry started. "How is it possible for a born-again Christian to work for a brutal dictator like Saddam?"

"Well, when Saddam offers you a job, it is difficult to refuse," replied Nabil gently. "Georges is often here with us, and I wish you could ask him for yourself. But at the moment he is in London, seeking to negotiate safe haven for Saddam if he chooses to flee the country."

"This is hard to comprehend," said Terry, looking over at Joel. Even his usually understated assistant was wide-eyed and looked astonished.

"Yes, but Saddam is Sunni, you see, and most Iraqis are Shia, so he does not trust them," explained Nabil. "But he trusts Christians, because he knows they will not try to kill him. He has sixty-eight palaces, and he is always moving about for his safety. He employs only Christians in the palaces, and makes sure to include a few, like my father-in-law, on his senior staff. They cannot refuse."

Terry paused for a moment, wondering if he should ask the question that had arisen in his mind. Would he regret it later if he did? *Go ahead*, urged the inner voice. But for once he wasn't sure if God was speaking to him or if the adrenalin rush of the past year had become an addiction. *No harm in asking.*

"Nabil, do you think your father-in-law could get me into Iraq?"

"It might be possible," replied Nabil, with a smile. "Americans generally are not allowed entry these days, but I would welcome the company."

After dinner, the three men went to Terry's room. A moment later, Nabil was exchanging telephone pleasantries with General Sada, while Terry and Joel sat on the two beds and listened to half of the conversation, which took place in English.

"There is an American minister with me, who has been helping

Afghan refugees," said Nabil. "He wants to go to Baghdad, to see what work God might have for him there. He asks if you are willing to obtain permission."

There was silence for a few moments, and then Nabil nodded.

"Yes. Yes sir, he is...." Then a pause. "Let me ask him."

Nabil covered the receiver with his hand and turned to Terry.

"He asked me if you are a good man and I said yes," said Nabil. "He says he will try, but that you will need to go as a member of the press. He wants to know if you can obtain credentials."

"Sure," replied Terry, nodding vigorously. He had no idea how or where he could get a reporter's badge, but there had to be a way.

A few days after the New Year, Terry, Joel and Nabil landed in Baghdad. The photo badge dangling from the lanyard around Terry's neck had come from a Tulsa TV station. Amazingly, his permission to enter Iraq had come straight from Saddam himself.

"The General assumed that Saddam must have been eager to approve an American reporter who dares to defy President Bush's restrictions," Nabil whispered as the three men exited their taxi and walked into the Al Rasheed Hotel in downtown Baghdad.

Terry started toward the check-in desk, but stopped dead in his tracks. Directly in front of him, a giant portrait of President George Bush dominated the lobby floor. At once he understood: The bottom of the foot was the lowest part of the human body in Eastern cultures, and walking across that painting meant paying the President a grave insult. This was undoubtedly Saddam's work.

Terry strode carefully around the painting and checked in, before joining Joel and Nabil to deliver food to a needy Christian family. Iraqis were suffering widespread shortages, but Terry suspected that here again their dictator was trying to gin up anger against America.

The Iraqi couple and their two children welcomed their guests and immediately began preparing a meal for everyone from their new provisions. Then, after dinner, they all sat down in the living room to talk of God's goodness. Terry listened at first, and then asked a question he had wondered about for weeks.

"What do Christians here in Iraq think of Saddam Hussein?"

Jumping up from their sofa, the husband and wife rushed to close the heavy drapes that framed their windows, frantically waving their hands in a *shushing* motion as they moved. Terry looked about the newly dimmed room at his panicked hosts, all four of them now frozen with fear. He had seen that look only once in his life, back in 1968 in the Soviet Union, at Jon's secret prayer meeting. Clearly, his question had been a mistake.

Quietly, Nabil leaned toward Terry, touching a finger to his ear and then pointing around the room. *House might be bugged*, he was saying. Then he pointed to his shoes and saluted. *They are listening for the sound of boots outside.*

As he and Nabil left an hour later, Terry whispered his apologies, and silently chided himself that night at the hotel. Still feeling chastened the next morning, he went with Nabil to the second stop of their mission: the Saddam Hussein Children's Hospital.

Terry extended his hand to the hospital administrator as Nabil introduced him.

"Dr. Law is an American minister and he is very concerned for...."

"Murderers!" yelled the administrator, as he hastily withdrew his hand. "Saddam has exposed your country's crimes. You have purposely withheld food and medicine for these children who are dying with cancer. You are to blame for all of this!"

The white sleeves of the administrator's lab coat flapped as he gestured grandly towards the wards on either side. Terry could see that the man's anguish was real. He obviously believed every word he was saying.

"Sir, this isn't true," said Terry quietly. "I don't expect you to believe me, but I promise you that I will learn the facts about this, and then I will return with as many medical supplies as I can bring. Please make a list of everything your hospital needs, and I will do my best."

Back in Tulsa, it didn't take long to find out the truth. Saddam had received $39 billion worth of food and medicine from the U.S. in exchange for oil, only to sell it all on the European black market in order to beef up his military and line his own pockets. Then he had blamed America for the shortages and proclaimed himself a hero, even renaming the children's hospital after himself, while leaving its hundreds of young patients to die.

At once, Terry began calling on donors, drug companies and suppliers, and by March he had amassed more than $500,000 worth of donated supplies. But America was now at war with Saddam, and once again, Terry found himself glued to the television, day after day, waiting for his chance to return.

* * *

At last, on May 1, President Bush announced victory and within the week Terry, his two sons, Scot and Jason, and Joel were in Amman, shaking hands with General Sada. Terry could see now why Nabil had wanted them to meet. Within minutes they were chatting like old friends.

"I have arranged for us to join a convoy that will take us across the desert to Baghdad," said the General. "It is dangerous, but I have been told that several properties I own are damaged and I need to inspect them. If you wish to go, I will take you."

The next day, Terry headed straight for the American Embassy in downtown Amman.

"This is crazy," scolded the Ambassador. "A German car was ambushed and riddled with bullets on that route just yesterday. Everyone survived, but they're lucky. You will probably die if you do this."

"I understand sir," said Terry. "But I've brought more than half a million dollars worth of medicine and hospital supplies, and I've got a promise to keep. I'm going."

The next morning, Terry and his crew climbed into the back of a white Chevy Suburban, their luggage stowed behind them, next to a large tank filled with gasoline. He watched as Joel carefully loaded the medical cargo into one of four other white Suburbans.

Twenty minutes later the five identical SUVs headed east toward the desert, joining seven more in a V-formation as soon as they had sped past the abandoned border station.

"The saddle tanks will enable us to make the 400-mile trip very quickly without stopping," explained Georges.

Less than five hours later, Terry saw smoke rising in the distance. Gradually, the tops of buildings broke the horizon. The convoy was already nearing the liberated Baghdad.

"Congratulations," said the General cheerily. "You four are the first American civilians to enter the free Iraq!"

Soon, Terry was unpacking his bags in a room at the Palestine Hotel, battered by the war, but still standing. Looking down from his window onto Firdos Square, he could see Saddam's decapitated statue lying twenty feet from its base, both body and head unmoved from where they had been separated a few days earlier at the hands of American troops. Dotting the horizon, plumes of gray smoke marked spots where buildings once had stood. He hoped the children's hospital was not among them.

An hour later, Terry's SUV pulled into the drive in front of the undamaged hospital, and within moments he was standing in the startled administrator's office.

"I am here to keep my promise," said Terry, as Joel and his sons began covering the floor in front of his desk with boxes labeled "chemotherapy."

The administrator stared at the labels for a moment...and then began to cry.

"I did not think you would return," he said. "I don't know what to say."

"We did not come to Iraq to kill your children, like Saddam told you on TV," said Terry, quietly. "We've come to heal them in Jesus' name. Please accept these gifts from us as Christians who believe that Jesus is the Son of God."

Back at his hotel, Terry sat in the lobby with Georges, rejoicing over today's success at the hospital. But the General offered only a wan smile in response.

"I have you to thank for this, Georges," said Terry. "But you look troubled. What is it?"

General Sada shifted uncomfortably in his seat. "I have returned to a land in ruins," he replied. "Today, while you were at the children's hospital, I went to my home, and found five gigantic fractures in the walls. My house is ruined, and most of the others that I own are in the same condition. My country is gone."

In his enthusiasm, Terry had forgotten that today was the General's first time to see Baghdad since before the war. Not knowing what to say, he looked at his new friend and silently prayed. Almost at once, he felt an urge to speak.

"Georges, Iraq is about to rise from the ashes, and you're going to be one of the main players in the new government," said Terry, his spine starting to tingle. "I know it seems unlikely now, and I don't know why I'm so sure of this, but you are going to represent God in the midst of Nebuchadnezzar's Babylon."

The General lifted his shoulders and raised his eyebrows, realizing that Terry had quite likely spoken a word from above.

"Did you know that Saddam considers himself Nebuchadnezzar reincarnated?" asked the General, his countenance brightening. "The ruins of Babylon are just a short distance from here, near his main palace."

* * *

It was as if the heavens had opened a month later when Terry's telephone rang at home in Tulsa. It was the General.

"Terry, Ambassador Bremer has appointed me as Iraq's new Minister of Defense!" said Georges proudly. "And he has appointed my Kurdish friend, Jalal Talabani, as the new President. Even better, Kurdistan will be allowed to function autonomously, almost like its own country!"

* * *

Over the next year, Terry received favor everywhere he went, even helping to plant a church in Irbil, the capital of Kurdistan, where Nabil often worked. For fourteen centuries, there had been no sizable Christian congregation anywhere in the Islamic world. But the Kurdzman Church quickly grew to several hundred new converts, and began planting branch churches in other cities. Soon their fairly new building in Irbil could only hold their burgeoning leadership. When he returned there in June 2004 to speak for a conference with more than 600 attendees, news crews from all four Arab television networks were filming the historic gathering.

"Nabil, I'm not sure I feel safe knowing Al Jazeera and the other networks are here," confided Terry, before preaching on the final evening. "How widely have they been reporting?"

"All over the Middle East," replied Nabil, as if he thought Terry must have known. "But President Barzani knows this, and he is providing his three cars and personal bodyguards to take you to the Baghdad airport tomorrow. You will be well protected."

Feeling reassured, Terry preached with all his heart to the large gathering of converted Muslims, most of whom claimed to have come to Christ because Jesus had appeared to them in visions or dreams. But his confidence was short lived. As soon as the meeting had finished, Nabil pulled him aside.

"Terry, the President's staff received a tip this evening," he whispered. "Al Qaeda has been watching, and they are waiting in ambush for you on the road to Baghdad. You must leave another way. President Barzani has arranged a taxi to take you north to the border of Turkey. Then you must switch to a Turkish taxi, and fly home from Diyarbakir."

For the first time since being attacked at the refugee camp two years earlier, Terry knew he was facing certain death. Leaving Irbil before dawn the next morning, he arrived at the Turkish border shortly before 10 a.m. The line of waiting taxis stretched hundreds of yards, and he offered $125 to the first driver to answer him in English.

By noon, he was across the border and speeding through the Turkish countryside.

"Excuse me," said Terry about an hour later, as he spotted a hotel in the center of one of the larger towns. "Toilet. Please, I need to stop."

The driver obliged and Terry sauntered up the steps of the rundown hotel. Two minutes later he trotted back down the same steps, but stopped dead before reaching the bottom. The driver had opened his rear door and was holding a large plastic bag he had retrieved from beneath Terry's seat. Startled by the sudden thud of shoes on the stairs behind him, he wheeled around to see he had been caught red-handed. Now he wore a look of pure hatred.

O Lord, heroin! thought Terry as his mind raced to grasp his predicament. *I've been sitting right on top of it all along. If we had gotten caught at the border, he would have blamed me, and I'd already be in jail.*

Terry knew what happened to westerners caught with drugs in Turkey: no trial, a life of torture in prison, with no chance of parole. At least he was still a free man, but what should he do now? He had to find a way to get back to the U.S.

Be bold, Terry told himself. Walking briskly back to the car as if he had seen nothing, he climbed into the front seat and motioned for the driver to go. *At least if he tries anything, I can defend myself better up here.*

The taxi soon entered a mountain pass, and while the driver navigated the twists and turns, Terry mentally rehearsed his moves, in case this drug runner took an unexpected detour.

Block with your left arm, while reaching past him for the door handle with your right hand. Yank it open, shove him out, and hit the gas.

He was ready.

A short while later the driver's cell phone rang, and he handed it to Terry. "For you," he said.

Bewildered and suspicious, Terry held the phone to his ear.

"You want to buy ticket?" said a woman's voice in thick, guttural English.

"No, I have a ticket. Thanks anyway," answered Terry, quickly handing the phone back to the driver. The man listened for a moment, then slammed the phone down on the seat beside him and looked at Terry with flashing eyes. On through the mountains the taxi drove, the driver becoming more agitated by the minute.

Offer him $300, said a voice in Terry's mind. *Do it now.*

Without second-guessing himself, Terry withdrew three hundreds from his pocket and fanned them out in front of the driver.

"I want to show my appreciation."

The driver looked at the bills and in an instant his frown became a toothy grin. The ploy had worked.

After finally reaching Diyarbakir and flying on to Istanbul that night, Terry checked in at the airport hotel and collapsed into bed. His arduous escape from Iraq had lasted eighteen exhausting hours. He was sound asleep at a little past midnight when his ringing cell phone jerked him awake.

What in the world is it now?

Rolling over in the darkness, Terry flipped open the phone.

"Terry, it's Don Moen," said a familiar voice. "What were you doing this afternoon at 4:30 Iraq time? Don't ask why—just tell me."

Terry was groggy, and Don's insistence only added to his confusion.

"Uh...let's see. At 4:30 this afternoon...Right about then, I was in a taxi being driven by a drug runner through the mountains of eastern Turkey, preparing to defend my life," said Terry with sudden clarity.

On the other end of the call, Don burst into laughter and quickly repeated Terry's words to his wife, Laura, who let out a shriek of joyful relief.

"Don, what's going on?" asked Terry. "Why were you so specific about 4:30?"

"Terry, it was 8:30 in the morning here in Alabama, and Laura and I were having breakfast with Steve and Ann Merkel. We were swapping old Living Sound stories with one another, and Steve mentioned you. As soon as he said your name, something inside me said we had to get down on our knees right there in the kitchen and pray for you, because you were in danger."

Don was laughing again.

"Can you believe it, Terry? Can you believe it?"

"For once, I'm glad you guys started telling stories about me," said Terry. "And praise God you know how to hear the Holy Spirit. Maybe I'll be able to get a good night's sleep after this. I'll call you when I get back to Tulsa."

Had he feared the television cameras back in Irbil enough to water down his message, Terry might have left Iraq in quiet safety, but he would also have left it in spiritual ignorance. So he had honored the name of Jesus by proclaiming it and stirring up a storm, knowing that God would honor that name and deliver him to safety.

Looking back on the drama after he returned home, it would have been easy for Terry to decide against going back to Iraq anytime soon. Al Qaeda obviously knew his name and what he looked like. But he *had* to return, because last week in Irbil, for the second time in two years, someone had asked him for help and he had made a vow. And now, he had to keep it.

CHAPTER 14

THE ACCIDENTAL
AMBASSADOR

IT WAS BARELY PAST daybreak on August 3, 2005, and the morning sun had already resumed baking the city of Baghdad. Shaking off the stiffness of two days of flying, Terry crawled out of bed and flipped on the ceiling fan at General Sada's borrowed home. Far more than an 8-hour time change, the biggest question he had faced in 41 years of ministry had kept him awake for much of the night.

How can an American Christian convince a Muslim nation to rewrite its constitution?

Twice in the past two years Terry had faced that question, most recently during last year's conference in Irbil, when a Catholic nun from Mosul had asked for help.

"I am Mother Catherine," she had said. "Nabil has helped my orphanage in Mosul, but I need your help for something different."

The fiftyish woman had spoken in a soft voice befitting her profession, but Terry could see that her eyes were full of resolve.

"Dr. Law, as you know, our nation is in the process of rebuilding its foundations," she had begun. "But Iraq's new constitution is being drafted with no provision for religious freedom. Without it we Christians will suffer."

Uh oh, I know where this is headed, Terry told himself.

"You must help us. We appreciate America's assistance, but we cannot rely on diplomats to solve spiritual problems."

The sister's words had eerily echoed the whispers of an Afghan Supreme Court justice the previous summer at a safe house in Kabul, Afghanistan.

"I have been a follower of Jesus for 19 years since hearing the gospel on radio," the justice had said. "But in all that time I have never encountered another Afghan believer, nor can I tell anyone of my faith in Christ. Now, we are about to defeat the Taliban, and soon we will ratify a new constitution. We need an article guaranteeing religious freedom, and I hope to see the United Nations Universal Declaration of Human Rights formally recognized. But it will take America's help, and you are the only American I have met. May I depend on you?"

The question had left Terry nearly speechless, and after returning to his hotel that night in 2003 he had packed his bags in a daze.

Lord, you've led me and taught me how to declare the gospel, face persecution, feed the poor and pray for the sick, but how can I ever hope to influence the government of a nation—one that's opposed to Christianity to begin with?

Terry had shared his dilemma with Larry Dalton two evenings later after flying to Vienna for a short reunion tour in Europe.

"Why don't you ask John Ashcroft?" Larry had suggested. "I played the concert for his inaugural celebration last year after he was sworn in as President Bush's Attorney General. We've been friends for a long time."

At once, Larry had dialed Ashcroft's office in Washington, D.C., and then handed the phone to Terry. To his shock, the secretary already knew who he was—"Larry has told me so many Living Sound stories!"—and promised to ask her boss for advice right away.

"Petitions," she'd said when she called back a couple of hours later. "The A.G. says that as a government we can't meddle with another country's constitutional process. However, a grassroots petition would carry a lot of weight with Afghanistan's leadership, because they're heavily indebted to the good will of the American people. You need to obtain as many signatures as you can."

Terry had vigorously followed the Attorney General's advice in the months that followed, eventually amassing more than 16,000 signed petitions. Then in December, the Afghan ambassador himself had delivered them to Afghanistan's new president, Hamid Karzai. Best of all, the human rights declaration had been included—translated word for word from Terry's petition—in the new Afghan Constitution ratified in January.

Five months later, Terry had met Mother Catherine. Had she somehow gotten news of his unlikely accomplishment?

"Will you be our intercessor, Dr. Law? Will you ask our government to include a guarantee of religious freedom in Iraq's new constitution, and to specify the right of all Iraqis to embrace the religion of their choice?"

"I'm just a preacher from Oklahoma," Terry had replied. "What can I do?"

"I understand," the sister had said. "But I believe our Father in heaven will give you the grace to make a difference. We really have no one else to help us."

That had been Catherine's trump card. Sipping his morning tea here at Georges' house, he remembered how she had locked eyes with him, silently refusing to take no for an answer.

"I will do my best, Mother," Terry had eventually promised. "I vow to you—I will do my best."

And over the past year he had kept his word. Nearly 20,000 signed petitions sitting under armed guard down the hall proved it.

"Good morning, my brother!" called General Sada's ever cheerful voice outside Terry's closed door. "Let us take our breakfast with Joel and then we will go to visit some dignitaries. This afternoon we will meet with President Talabani, and tomorrow is the big one with Prime Minister al Jaafari."

Finally, thought Terry. His meeting with Ibrahim al Jaafari had almost taken place in June. Terry had gotten as far as Heathrow Airport in London when his cell phone rang.

"Terry, this is Georges. I'm sorry, but your meeting with the Prime Minister must be postponed. He has just left Baghdad to meet with President Bush."

Terry had stood there in the vast hallway connecting Heathrow's terminals, wondering what to do next, when his phone rang again.

White House, said the caller I.D. on the phone's outer screen.

Oh, come on, he'd thought, as he flipped it open. *Somebody's playing with me.*

"Hello?"

"Is this Dr. Terry Law?" said an unfamiliar female voice. She sounded young.

"Yes, who's calling?"

"Dr. Law, my name is Meghan O'Sullivan. I am President Bush's Deputy National Security Advisor on Iraq and Afghanistan. I understand you are on the ground in both of those countries. Is it possible for you to come to the White House?"

This couldn't be happening. George Bush's assistant was calling him?

"Uh, yes ma'am. When would you like me to come? I'm in London at the moment."

"Can you be here in two days?"

"Yes, yes. I'll be there."

Terry had stood there reeling. Ten minutes earlier he had been on his way to Baghdad, then back to Tulsa, and now he was headed for the White House.

Lord, I don't know what's happening, he had prayed as he re-arranged his plans. *But obviously you've got a better one than ours.*

Two days later in Washington, D.C., Terry had shown Meghan one of the petitions he had prepared for the Iraqi Prime Minister.

"This is wonderful, Dr. Law," she had responded. "Please keep going forward on this. As you know, our Government can't tell them what to put in there, so as a citizen you actually have more influence on the process than I. But please call me regularly while you're over there, and I can advise you while you're on the ground."

Rescheduling his appointment with Prime Minister al Jaafari had been easy, now that Georges had been appointed the P.M.'s National Security Advisor, and looking back over the past two months, Terry marveled at how God had so precisely reordered his schedule.

Maybe one small person can make a difference after all, he told himself as he walked down the hall to the dining room.

A few minutes later, Terry and Joel finished their breakfast while General Sada readied his convoy of Land Cruisers for the perilous commute into central Baghdad. Once inside the Green

Zone they would be safe, but until then they would be running another gauntlet of red lights.

It was late in the afternoon when Terry finished his other appointments and finally arrived at President Jalal Talabani's residence. The two men observed protocol with an exchange of gifts—Terry a cowboy hat and big-buckle belt, and Talabani a sandalwood chess set—and then proceeded to the business at hand. The Iraqi President was a friendly, rotund man. He might have limited executive authority, but Terry knew that his endorsement would add extra weight when he presented a sample petition to the Prime Minister the next day.

The jovial Kurdish politician scanned the document, then rolled back his head and gave a big laugh.

"This is wonderful," he exclaimed. "You are quite bold! I will add my recommendation for approval when it is time to vote."

The appointment was brief and soon it was time to leave. To Terry's surprise, President Talabani insisted on walking his guests outside. But as soon as the door opened, and a dozen cameras began whirring, the Iraqi's reason became apparent: An American Christian minister had come to Iraq for high level meetings about the nation's new constitution, and Talabani, as a Kurd, was using the occasion to make a statement.

Terry looked at the raft of microphones standing a few feet away, between him and the nearest Land Cruiser. Just as in Irbil, all four Arab television networks were present, but this time they were yelling questions in English.

"Why is a Christian minister visiting the President of Iraq, sir?" they all seemed to be asking at once.

Terry remembered having to flee for his life after the last time he had faced these cameras, and as the heat rose around his collar, he stepped back inside the door to speak with Georges.

"What do I do now?" he stage-whispered. "Is somebody trying to get me killed?"

"You have no choice, Terry," answered the General. "You must do the interview. I will interpret for you."

Reluctantly, Terry walked back outside to face the cameras. His heart was pounding, but at least having the National Security Advisor standing beside him was a comfort.

Lord, you've put this whole thing together, he prayed silently. *This moment can be a game changer for believers all over this nation. This moment, and my life, are in your hands.*

As soon as Terry stepped before the microphones, the question was renewed.

"Why is a Christian minister visiting with the President of Iraq, sir?"

Knowing that his words were being heard in several Muslim countries, Terry spoke deliberately.

"I am a follower of Jesus," he began, "and so are thousands of American soldiers who have risked their lives for the people of Iraq. Many of our young men and women have sacrificed their lives, so that the Iraqi people can live in freedom, including the freedom to worship God as they choose. I have come to ask that freedom of religion be included in your new Constitution."

A few additional questions were asked, but by comparison they were irrelevant. News had been made. Within minutes, the cameras were gone and the convoy was exiting the President's compound.

"Congratulations, my friend!" said General Sada, gesturing with uplifted hands.

"What for?" asked Terry in a weary voice. He suddenly felt exhausted.

"You have just become the most wanted man in Iraq, and I am the second because I interpreted for you!"

The General's words weighed heavily on Terry as he lay in bed that night, listening to the sounds of gunfire from downtown and hoping they would not grow closer. Had he been foolhardy or faithful before the cameras? Time would tell—soon.

The next day, when at last Terry stood in Prime Minister Ibrahim al Jaafari's spacious office, he was more than ready to finish his year long mission. With the constitutional convention only two weeks away, he knew the P.M.'s time would be limited.

"Too many Iraqi Christians' lives are on the line to waste time," he had told Joel on the way into town. "As soon as we finish the formalities, I'm getting down to business. Make sure the petitions are ready."

As he and Joel shook hands with the Prime Minister, Terry took in the grandeur of his surroundings, noting the fine Persian rug, gilded furniture, and the uniformed guards to either side of al Jaafari's desk. The only thing out of place was an extra man, a black-robed, black-bearded Muslim cleric sitting in the far corner of the room.

Probably just another advisor.

With the handshaking finished, the Prime Minister quickly came to the point, just as Terry had hoped.

"Why have you asked to see me, Dr. Law?" he asked in Arabic.

Terry looked at General Sada, who was interpreting. As al Jaafari's senior advisor, Georges was putting his career and, once again, his life on the line. Terry knew he needed to measure his words.

"Mr. Prime Minister, we Americans have sent our young people here to die for your freedom. Our own most sacred freedom is that of being able to choose our religion."

Terry pointed to the tall stack of petitions Joel had placed on the carpet.

"I have brought nearly 20,000 signed petitions from people in America, Canada, and England, calling upon your nation to include Article 18 of the United Nations Universal Declaration of Human Rights in your new Constitution. As you know, that article says everyone has the right to freedom of religion, and that this right includes freedom to change his religion or belief, and to practice that religion either in public or in private. Sir, I am specifically asking you to incorporate this declaration in the document."

The Prime Minister's mouth gaped slightly, and for a moment he looked at Georges, as if to say, *Why are you allowing me to be put on the spot like this?*

Terry stood in place, looking at the P.M. and waiting for a response. From the corner of his eye, he could see the General was waiting too.

Al Jaafari looked down and cleared his throat.

"I am an admirer of your U.S. Constitution, Dr. Law, and I know the importance your founders placed on religious freedom."

The Prime Minister gestured for his guests to be seated, and continued speaking while pacing the floor in front of them.

"Your John Adams..." he began. And on and on he spoke, of Adams, Washington, Jefferson, the Bill of Rights, various amendments, the separation of powers...Terry could see that this man clearly knew volumes about American government. But he wasn't answering the question.

He's posturing, Terry thought as he feigned attention. *Just biding his time until he can get us out of here.*

The clock ticked slowly. At last, 45 minutes after he had

launched into his lecture, al Jaafari paused long enough for Terry to speak.

"Georges, ask him if I can repeat my question."

The Prime Minister nodded, as if to say, *Of course.*

Terry stood to his feet, as did everyone else except the Imam in the corner.

"Mr. Prime Minister, thousands of young American men and women have sacrificed their lives so that your people can live freely and openly profess any religion they choose. Are you willing to incorporate Article 18 of the United Nations Universal Declaration of Human Rights into Iraq's new constitution?"

Again, al Jaafari looked down and began to pontificate while pacing the floor. After five more minutes, Terry looked at a clock on the wall. It was time to leave.

"Georges, that was a complete waste of time," said Terry as he and Joel followed General Sada back through the marble corridors and outside to the Land Cruiser.

"No, no, Terry, it was not," replied the General. "Did you notice the Imam sitting in the corner?"

"Yes," said Terry. "What about him?"

"He is the senior religious cleric of al Jaafari's political party, *al Dawa.* He knew why you were there and was listening to everything. That is why al Jaafari kept talking and talking without really answering you. It was too dangerous."

"So we might have a chance?"

"Oh yes. Yes, you will see. The Prime Minister did not say yes, but more importantly, he did not say no. Wait and see. We have a very good chance."

Three days later, Terry was back at Georges' damaged main residence. A dust storm had swept in from the Anbar Province earlier and plunged Baghdad into darkness. Terry was sitting in the living room, looking at the blanket of grit that had poured in through the concussion cracks in the wall, when Georges walked in.

"Terry, I just received a call from a Sunni sheik in Amman, Jordan," said Georges, holding up his cell phone. "He is one of the seven sheiks who are leading the resistance against our new government. I know them all because they were friends of Saddam. The sheik says they would like to invite you to Amman to meet with them on your way home to America."

"You're kidding me!" exclaimed Terry. "What would they want with me?"

"I don't know, but if you want to accept their invitation I will go with you."

"Give me their names and I'll call the White House."

Georges wrote the names on a piece of paper and Terry climbed two flights of stairs to join a sniper stationed on the roof. Stepping into a half inch of dust that looked like tan snow, he dialed the number Meghan O'Sullivan had given him two months earlier. Within moments she answered and Terry briefed her on his appointment with the Prime Minister, before bringing up his mysterious invitation to Amman.

"What do you think I should do?" Terry asked.

"Tell me their names and I'll check them against our list," she said.

Terry recited the list Georges had given him and listened as Meghan typed them into her computer. Then he heard her whistle.

"Terry, these men are all known terrorists and friends of Saddam," she said.

"Yes, I know. What is your recommendation?"

"If you go and see them, you'll be the next American on television, getting his throat cut. You absolutely do not have our permission to do this."

Terry was stunned by the severity of Meghan's warning, and waited a moment before replying.

"Thank you, Meghan. I'm still not sure what to do, but I'll pray about it and make my decision."

The phone call ended frostily, and Terry walked downstairs to rejoin Georges.

"The White House is mistaken," said Georges after Terry had filled him in. "If you accept the sheiks' hospitality, they will not kill you. It is not their way. I promise you, you will be safe."

Three evenings later, Terry stood on an immaculate lawn behind a luxurious suburban home in Amman, and marveled at the long feast-laden table before him. He looked at Joel, a few steps away, whose arched brows registered a silent whistle. Nearby, General Sada was making conversation in Arabic with the seven sheiks.

Everyone was seated, Terry and Joel at one end, while the General sat amongst the sheiks at the other to translate. Dinner had barely begun when suddenly a roar of laughter exploded at General Sada's end of the table. Already feeling apprehensive in his strange surroundings, Terry jumped.

"What's happening, Georges? What did you say?" he asked.

"I told them that the White House warned you not to come because these men would kill you," smiled Georges. Again the sheiks erupted with laughter, this time at the look on Terry's reddening face.

Earlier that day Terry had learned that the sheiks somehow thought he worked for President Bush. Now, that mistaken impression was undoubtedly making the joke sweeter for them.

After that, the conversation flowed more freely, and eventually Terry worked up the courage to ask a question that had puzzled him for three days.

"How did you know about me?"

"We have been watching you for some time," replied Terry's primary host. "We have seen what you do for the people of Iraq, and we decided that you are an American we can trust."

"Why did you want to me to come here?"

"We want to know what you Americans *really* want for our country's future."

Terry took a moment to consider his current predicament.

On one hand, I don't have any authority whatsoever to speak for George Bush. But on the other...they don't know that.

He thought of the thousands of Americans who had died, and the countless widows and orphans of Iraq, all casualties of the mutual hatred between Sunni and Shia, Iraq's two main Muslim groups. And here they stood, the commanders of more than 100,000 Sunni rebels who were fighting against the western Coalition, asking *him* about Iraq's future.

Terry looked up at seven of the world's "most dangerous terrorists" as they gathered around his chair, and quietly waited for him to speak. If ever he had been in the eye of the storm, this was it. The very calm in his spirit told him so.

Lord, will I ever be given such an open door for the cause of Christ again? He already knew the answer. *Go for it!*

"America wants peace for all Iraqis, for the Sunni, for the Shia, the Kurds, and Assyrians, and all the rest. We want your people to stop killing one another, to stop persecuting those of us who follow Jesus, and to let the land rest. America...America wants you to stop fighting the Coalition and join hands with us to defeat Osama bin Laden and al Qaeda."

Terry could hardly believe the words that were coming from his mouth, but knew he must not stop now.

"If you are willing to come to Washington—*dear Lord what am I saying?*—I believe I can arrange a meeting for you at the White House. But only if you are willing to stop fighting against us and fight with us, for the peace of Iraq."

* * *

A week later, Terry was at home in Tulsa, trying to figure out a palatable way to let Meghan O'Sullivan know what an outrageous step he had taken, when the headlines broke: Iraq's Transitional National Assembly had accepted a formal draft for the nation's new Constitution. The key provisions from his petition had been included in two of the document's articles.

The White House, pleased with the results of Terry's petition drive, expressed cautious optimism when he called with the news of his bold, unauthorized offer to the Sunni sheiks. But would he mind using his good favor with both sides of the Iraqi divide to do a bit of shuttle diplomacy?

"I'd be happy to," he said—but what else could he say?

"Lord, I have no idea how to be a diplomat," Terry often prayed after that. And he was right. The brassy, big-mouthed, preacher's kid from the prairies of Canada had given his life to God, but somehow kept his big mouth. He was good at taking chances. Preaching against Marx and Lenin in a Communist-owned nightclub. Telling a quarter million Roman Catholics in a field in Poland how to be born again. Facing down the Soviet KGB and walking out on an interrogation. Even speaking on behalf of the President before a gaggle of terrorists. Yeah, he could do those things.

But diplomacy?

2006 arrived and with it the specter of war returned to Iraq. Terry knew that soon after his visit to Amman, the seven sheiks had approved a new movement in Anbar Province, west of Baghdad. And as the year passed, their "Sunni Awakening" seemed at least to stanch some of the bloodshed there. Maybe his efforts had played a part.

Then, in November, America's national "midterm" elections were held, and widespread Republican defeat was hailed as a sign that President Bush's policies in Iraq were begin rejected. Less than two months later, Meghan O'Sullivan left her White House post, taking most of Terry's influence with her.

If there was one thing the past 18 months had taught Terry, however, it was that placing his life fully in God's hands had enabled him to stand at rest amidst the fiercest of storms. Life in the eye was the true place of peace, the place where "God's strength is made perfect in our weakness." And something inside him said that in having expended his best efforts, God's grace for Iraq somehow remained.

* * *

It was late summer 2007, months after Terry's last communication with the White House that a call came from Amman, Jordan: Iraq's 107,000 Sunni rebels had suddenly switched sides and joined President Bush's much maligned "surge." By the next new year, even the mainstream media were agreeing that the surge had worked. But Terry knew the truth.

God's grace alone had "worked" a victory for peace in Iraq. And only grace could keep it.

CHAPTER 15

OUT OF THE STORMS

IT WAS MONDAY, April 8, 2013, the 70th birthday of Terrance Herbert Law, and he had planned to celebrate it at home in Tulsa, with a house full of children and grandchildren turning the place upside down. But here he was—in Greece, of all places—standing and waiting in the arrivals terminal at Athens International.

This moment was the culmination of one of the most improbable events of Terry's whole life...

The previous seven years since the ratification of Iraq's new constitution had been shaky for the nation, but incredibly fruitful for Terry's ministry, World Compassion. Over that span they had doled out millions of dollars in food and medicine, and experienced the special joy of putting shoes on the feet of 50,000 Iraqi children. The Ayatollah of Baghdad had even given Terry permission to hand out an Arabic language picture Bible with each set of shoes, and as a result, new churches had been planted in villages and towns all over Iraq.

"Did you say *the Ayatollah of Baghdad*?" Jim had exclaimed one morning in 2008, after Terry called back to explain why he had just hung up on him twice in 10 minutes. His brand new iPhone had suddenly started blaring out the theme to *James Bond 007* – programmed by Terry's fun loving son-in-law, Matt—while he was talking on his home phone with the Ayatollah of Baghdad through an interpreter. He hadn't known how to silence the iPhone's ringer, so he had simply answered and hung up. Twice.

"The Ayatollah has given us permission to include picture Bibles with the backpacks and tennis shoes we're distributing to Iraqi children," Terry had told Jim. "We're using them to introduce the gospel to the kids' families, and then later we send Iraqi pastors back to their villages to preach and plant new churches. It's working great."

"Well, I guess an Ayatollah trumps *me*," laughed Jim, and the two men had moved on to discuss less weighty matters.

With the initial reduction in violence under Iraq's new government, Terry's ministry had soared, especially up north in Kurdistan, where the peace was holding steady.

"I would rather see a Kurd become a Christian than a radicalized Muslim any day," Kurdish Prime Minister Barzani had told the press not long before. The remark had provoked an assassination attempt two weeks later, but Barzani still refused to back down. After that, Terry had begun supporting a handful of emboldened ex-Muslim evangelists, among them an irrepressible Kurd he codenamed Pastor Jamal.

Over the next few years, Terry had worked often with Jamal. He especially relished going into the villages of Kurdistan with his gregarious friend, not only because Jamal loved sharing his faith, but also because, like Terry, he seemed to be missing his "fear" gene.

"Today's shipment of backpacks and shoes is ready to go, Dr. Terry," said Jamal on a spring morning in 2010. "Let's take them to the Catholic children's home near Mosul."

"That entire area is an al Qaeda stronghold," replied Terry. "Are you sure you want to go there?"

Jamal's voice grew impassioned.

"That is exactly why we must go. There are 100 children at that orphanage, and they are only there because al Qaeda killed their fathers. They need us."

Ninety minutes later Terry and Jamal arrived at the orphanage, with their distribution team and supply van in tow. Just as Jamal had said, the Sisters had assembled their young charges, who sat quiet and wide-eyed with anticipation.

Terry looked at the kids, their clothes tattered, their dirty feet clad either in rubber flip-flops or nothing at all. After all his years of coming to Iraq, he knew that most children here had never even *seen* a pair of shoes. He also knew what would happen as soon as the first few sets of durable white sneakers started to appear. Little hearts would be won, and young lives would be forever changed.

This is what he lives for, thought Terry as he watched Jamal sorting stacks of shoeboxes by gender and size. Having experienced several pre-adolescent riots on village streets, Jamal had arranged for the Sisters to call the children forward one by one, in order to match shoes with feet.

Just as Terry expected, the sight of each pair of white rubber soles brought gasps and giggles that gradually grew to a happy din. Before long, the nuns had ceased their efforts to stifle it. All around the room, boys and girls who had never worn shoes were taking their first, awkward steps, some of them pitching onto their knees from the unexpected traction, others sprinting back and forth like spring ponies. All but one little girl, who sat silent in her flip-flops beside a closed box.

"Jamal," said Terry, tugging on his colleague's sleeve. "Ask her why she isn't wearing her new shoes. Maybe they're the wrong size."

Jamal knelt beside the girl and spoke gently to her in Arabic, while Terry watched from a few feet away. At first her chin dropped when the big man approached, but as soon as he had asked the question, she placed her hand on the shoebox lid and looked up to answer. It was an earnest look that reminded Terry of his own Misty when she had been about seven.

Jamal's eyes were glistening when he rose to interpret.

"She says they're too beautiful, and she doesn't want to get them dirty."

Now Terry's own eyes dampened. For all of his hobnobbing with Presidents and Prime Ministers, moments like these rekindled the lamp in his soul that danger sometimes dimmed, and reminded him of why Jesus preferred the company of children to the fellowship of Pharisees. "Let the little children come to Me," the Lord had instructed his self-appointed bodyguards, "and do not forbid them; for of such is the kingdom of heaven."

The ride back to Irbil felt a little less bumpy that day, as Terry and Jamal quietly savored the small sea of calm they had discovered so near to Mosul's tempest. Yet danger was never far away, as another coworker, Aram, had reminded Terry two days earlier, after an outreach to a Yazidi village.

"Dr. Terry, while Jamal was preaching and I was handing food to villagers from the back of the truck, two young Kurds walked past us," Aram had said. "I overheard one say to the other, 'These are American infidels. If we kill them right now, we will have a straight path to heaven.'"

Terry looked over at Jamal, whose eyes were on the road. If he had been shaken by Aram's disclosure, he didn't show it. Even after several death threats, Jamal had gone on traveling and preaching.

At last the van pulled up to Terry's hotel, and after climbing out he leaned back into the passenger window to ask Jamal a question that had bothered him for several days.

"Every so often, you clutch at your head, Jamal. Is something wrong?"

"I have been having headaches, Dr. Terry," Jamal replied. "The pain comes suddenly, and it is so terrible...I don't know how to say the right word. Lately they are coming every day."

"It's okay, Jamal," said Terry. "We'll get you to a doctor in Jordan to find out what is wrong."

Terry was at home in Tulsa two weeks later when Nabil phoned from Amman.

"Jamal's brain scan revealed a tumor on the left side, but the doctor says he can use gamma rays to kill it," said Nabil. "They will do the treatment soon and send him home to Iraq in a few days."

Before long, Jamal was indeed back at home in Irbil, recovering and headache free. When Terry returned to northern Iraq a few months later, he was pleased to see his friend preaching Christ with more boldness and enthusiasm than ever. Kurdistan's virtual self-rule, and her government's dedication to religious and economic freedom, were causing the province to blossom in ways that were unimaginable anywhere else in Iraq.

That made Nabil's phone call to Tulsa the next July truly shocking.

"Terry, Jamal is in prison," said Nabil, his voice breaking. "The police took him from his home on July 6, and he is accused of spying for Iran."

"Nabil, that's absurd," exclaimed Terry, trying to grasp what he was hearing. "They couldn't have concocted a more ridiculous charge. This must be about his preaching."

"Yes, of course," said Nabil. "Recently some Yazidi elders complained to someone in Irbil. But there is no trial scheduled and the authorities will tell us nothing more."

As soon as Terry had hung up the phone, he dialed General Sada.

"Georges, please send a message to Prime Minister Barzani," asked Terry. "Tell him these are false charges and ask that Jamal be released at once."

The General readily consented and sent the message, but after several days, there had been no response. A second message was dispatched and phone calls were made. Weeks went by and more pleas were sent. Months passed, and still there was silence. Most mysterious of all, no charges had been filed, and no trial date set.

Perhaps a letter from a United States senator would carry more weight, thought Terry. He called Oklahoma's senior Senator, James Inhofe, a former Tulsa mayor and good friend, whose sterling record on human rights was internationally respected. The Senator quickly agreed and sent a letter, but still there was no reply.

Charges were filed finally in late 2012, but no trial date was set.

"Terry, we've received some bad news from Iraq," said Joel one morning in January 2013. "Jamal has been admitted to the prison hospital with severe headaches."

"Oh no," Terry grimaced. "If another tumor is growing it could mean the cancer has returned. And in an Iraqi prison hospital? Jamal could die and they wouldn't care."

Go—Go now.

There it was, yet again, that word *Go*. For 18 months Terry had waited to hear this word. He had wanted so badly to travel to Iraq and intercede in Jamal's behalf, and even his closest friends had questioned his seeming inaction. But like St. Paul wanting to go to Asia, he had known that he must wait. Now, in a flash, he knew with unbridled certainty that somehow he was going to save a man's life. St. Paul had called it the gift of faith—not just the confidence and trust in God common to all believers, but a unique, perfectly timed flourish of grace that sweeps across the soul and erases all thoughts of failure, no matter how daunting the odds.

"Joel, get us tickets to Irbil," said Terry. "Tell Nabil to meet us in Amman. We're going to go get Jamal out of prison."

On February 18, the three landed in Irbil.

"Terry, a local friend just told me you were the front page story in the newspaper this morning," said Nabil, after they had settled in at their hotel. "The whole city knows you are here to obtain freedom for an ex-Muslim Christian who is accused of spying for Iran."

"Then let's make some more news," said Terry. Never in his life had he felt more certain that he was doing the will of God.

After waving a second, hand-signed letter from Senator Inhofe in the faces of a few bureaucrats the next day, Terry quickly gained permission to see Jamal. With the help of American Consul General Paul Sutphen, he secured an appointment with Kurdistan's Deputy Prime Minister, Karim Sinjari.

Arriving at the prison that afternoon with Joel and Nabil, Terry was relieved to discover a clean looking facility and a friendly warden, who quickly escorted his guests to his outer office.

"I will send a guard to bring the prisoner to you," said the warden.

Five minutes later a haggard-looking Jamal walked into the room, looking as if he were puzzled by his summons. But as his eyes landed, his countenance changed.

"Terry Law! *Terry Law!*" he yelled, running across the warden's office with his arms wide. "You come back—you come *back*!"

Grabbing Terry in a ferocious bear hug, the gaunt prisoner lifted him off the floor. "You came for me," he sobbed.

Terry was shedding his own tears as Jamal lowered him to the floor. "May we have some privacy?" he asked the warden, who nodded and quietly opened the door to his private quarters.

"Get your camera ready to record some evidence," Terry whispered to Joel as he escorted Jamal into the warden's elaborate office. After all four men had entered, Nabil closed the door.

Terry held out a chair for his friend, but as Jamal started to move, his body stiffened and he staggered back, then willed himself forward to fall onto the table. Terry and Joel lunged simultaneously to soften his fall, and Nabil quickly joined in to pray.

Within a couple of minutes, the worst of Jamal's pain had subsided, and Terry knew that he should debrief him without delay.

"Have you been mistreated?"

He had been tortured, Jamal said. An interrogator had clapped his ears until they bled, and left him tied up for hours between the hot air exhausts on the giant air-conditioning units in the prison courtyard. With summer temperatures averaging 120 degrees, Terry knew that the even hotter blasts from those vents could bake a man's skin.

"At first I suffered, but then I began to sing," said Jamal, "and as I raised my voice to praise God, a coolness came upon me. I didn't feel the heat anymore. Instead, I felt as if I were floating in a cool river. And I was not burned.

"After ten days, they made me sign a paper, but by then I could no longer see. I do not know what I signed."

Terry asked more questions, and then Joel and Nabil joined him again to pray for Jamal. After an hour, it was time to leave.

By the time he got back to his room that afternoon, Terry was burning with anger. He knew that he needed to prepare for his morning appointment with the Deputy P.M., but he struggled as he tried to rehearse the day's events and make his notes.

Someone thinks he'll get away with killing a good man, thought Terry. *But not this time. Not Jamal.*

Before going to sleep that night, Terry followed his suffering friend's example and began praising God. This was another storm, and like all the others over the years, there would be no running from it. He knew now that God's power to calm the storm was always *in its eye*, not on some safe, distant shore.

By the time Terry walked into Deputy Prime Minister Sinjari's office at ten o'clock the next morning, pouring out his complaint in praise had actually tempered his resolve even more.

"Have you seen this, sir?" Terry asked, after the formalities had ended. He handed Sinjari the letter from Senator Inhofe.

The look on the Minister's face answered the question before he spoke.

"I have never seen this letter," he said. "Please sit down."

Until that moment, Terry had known Sinjari was wary of him. Why was this American clergyman advocating for an Iranian spy? But the letter had changed everything.

"Dr. Law, are you here only for humanitarian reasons?" asked the Minister.

"Yes, sir. My friend Jamal has a cancerous brain tumor and needs to receive treatment not available in Iraq. I believe he is innocent of the charges, and is being persecuted solely for practicing his Christian faith."

As Terry spoke, it was plain to see that none of his pleas from the past year and a half—not even Senator Inhofe's letter—had ever reached their intended recipients. It was obvious as well, that Minister Sinjari sincerely wanted to uphold Kurdistan's much heralded policy of religious freedom.

Terry knew it was time to make his case.

"Sir, just imagine if, instead of keeping Jamal in prison and arousing the ire of the entire Christian world in the west, you were to set him free. Think of the good will that would be engendered if Senator Inhofe were to tell Capitol Hill that Kurdistan's government had pardoned an ex-Muslim who had converted to Christianity, and released him to live in the West."

The Deputy Prime Minister's eyebrows raised, and he sat silently for a moment.

"Dr. Law, you must realize that here in Kurdistan, our Executive Branch cannot overrule the courts. Whoever brought the case would have to reopen it, and that will simply not be possible."

Sinjari paused, as though considering whether or not he should say whatever it was he was thinking. Finally, he spoke.

"However...there is one possibility. We have a provision called Private Amnesty," he said. "It is not the prerogative of our Prime Minister, Nechirvan Barzani, but of our President, Massoud Barzani."

Terry recognized the name. The P.M.'s uncle was not only the provincial President, but also patriarch of one of the two most powerful tribes in Kurdistan.

"Dr. Law," Sinjari continued. "Private Amnesty exists, but it has never been granted."

Terry listened, inwardly checking his faith. The flame that had been lit in his spirit a week ago back home in Tulsa was not even flickering. Somehow, he knew that he knew: Jamal would be set free.

"What will you need from me?" Terry asked, sounding confident. It was obvious he had won Minister Sinjari's respect and trust. He needed to keep this ball rolling.

"I will obtain the prisoner's latest x-rays and medical evaluation," answered Sinjari. "You will need to get a letter from Jamal himself, addressed to the President, formally requesting Private Amnesty. I will keep the letter from your Senator, and put it with the documents you send to me."

"Where is President Barzani now?" asked Terry.

"He is in Moscow, negotiating an oil contract with Russian President Vladimir Putin," said Sinjari. "I will give the necessary documents to him when he returns next week."

While Terry wrote memos, the Deputy Prime Minister explained more details and made phone calls, pressing his staff into action. Clearly, he was a man of his word.

Terry looked at his watch. "Expect ten minutes," someone had said the day before. But an hour had passed and Sinjari was still working.

At last it was time to leave, and as he shook hands with the Deputy Prime Minister, Terry knew he was bidding farewell to a friend.

"Dr. Law, there is one more provision," said Sinjari. "Jamal must also promise to leave Iraq and never come back."

Terry nodded. He already knew that Jamal would never again

be safe in his homeland. "Thank you, sir. I can assure you of his cooperation," he said.

Terry and Joel returned to Tulsa and waited, Karim Sinjari having told them they would probably receive the President's decision soon after he returned from Russia the following week. But the week passed, as did the rest of February, and then March.

It was Easter Sunday afternoon, the last day of March, when Terry's cell phone rang during his layover at the airport in Dallas.

"Terry, I've got good news," said Joel. "Jamal was freed from prison at 3:30 this afternoon, Iraqi time. They drove him to the door of his home and released him into the care of his wife and children."

"Hallelujah!" yelled Terry at the top of his voice as he walked through the busy airport concourse. At least a hundred fellow travelers froze in their steps, but he couldn't have cared less.

"Hallelujah!"

All at once, Terry's brain began to fire.

"Joel, send Nabil to Iraq, and get Jamal and his family out of that house into a safe location," he said. "Tell him to put them in a good hotel until I can figure out what to do."

And so it was that a week later, on his 70th birthday, Terry was in Greece, wondering what his loved ones were up to back at home while he stood here, waiting at the Athens airport with another friend, Pastor Sameh, and Jamal's oldest daughter, Amira, who had taken refuge in the U.S. Would his family have the cake without him, or save it until he got home?

Terry had not yet realized that in completing one type of Jubilee, he was commencing another. For in finishing his 70th year of life, he was also starting his 50th year in ministry. And as Jesus had said in Luke, chapter 4, the real purpose of Jubilee was to "preach the gospel to the poor...to heal the brokenhearted... to proclaim liberty to the captives and recovery of sight to the blind...to set at liberty those who are oppressed...to proclaim the acceptable year of the Lord."

The green lane marking the Customs exit at Athens International was crowded with a wave of new arrivals that Monday afternoon when Terry first spotted the shock of thick black hair crowning Jamal's handsome tan face. The happy Iraqi was craning his neck to see above the crowd, while Nabil and Jamal's wife Amina steered their three younger children through the crush of arriving passengers.

As he walked out into the terminal where the crowd fanned out, Jamal's face suddenly brightened and he broke into a full gallop.

"Dr. Terry! Dr. Terry, we did it!" he exulted, gripping Terry yet again in a bear hug. "We are free!"

Then, slowly and without relaxing his embrace, Jamal sank to his knees and wept.

"Thank you, Dr. Terry. Thank you," he sobbed.

Moved deeply himself, Terry felt more than a little conspicuous, with Jamal's arms wrapped around his legs, his heaving cries threatening to topple him to the floor like Saddam's statue.

"Come, let's go celebrate," said Terry in an effort at self-rescue. "Let's get you checked into your hotel and have a long celebration."

"It is Dr. Law's birthday," chimed in Pastor Saleh, a fellow immigrant whose ministry in a neighboring country would find a permanent home for the family after Terry's departure in two days.

Jamal was smiling and still wiping his eyes as he rose to his feet.

"Yes, we must celebrate your birthday and our freedom. We must praise God!" he said, half-laughing.

The early morning series of flights had taken their toll and after a quick debriefing at their hotel, the happy travelers collapsed into bed. Terry's birthday celebration would have to take place later that evening than planned.

It was nearing 9 p.m. when the party assembled in a private, second-story room at the restaurant Pastor Saleh had arranged, and Terry was eager to hear everything from Jamal that he must have held back in the warden's office five weeks earlier.

"Jamal, were you able to minister to other prisoners?" inquired Terry.

The Kurd's face brightened.

"Oh, yes. I was blessed to lead twenty-six Muslims to Jesus during my time there," said Jamal. "Even on the day that I saw you, after you left—you remember, I was in great pain."

Terry nodded for his friend to continue.

"All I could think about was returning to my bed, but on my way another prisoner stopped me. 'I have watched your life in here, Jamal, and I want to know the peace you have,' he said. So I decided I must tell him about Jesus, and as soon as I began, the pain in my head went away.

"Dr. Terry, I led him to Jesus after you left the prison! Maybe he would not know the Lord if you had gotten me freed earlier."

Terry marveled yet again at the courage of his friend, an unassuming, real-live hero. And as one might expect of a man commemorating 70 extraordinary years, he remembered other heroes as well.

His father, Bert, the Superman of his youth.

Dwight McLaughlin, who had planted within him a vision,

and Pastor Whittle, who had rescued it.

Oral Roberts, who had taught him to pursue the storms that others fled.

An aging Cardinal who had opened Poland to him, and a young Pope who had opened the world.

Jon Karner, who had risked his freedom, and Viktor, who had sacrificed his own.

General Sada, who had taken Terry into hell's furnace.

Jamal, who had come through its fire.

Never another Murray Ingham, he had promised God half a century ago. *Never another soul I let slip through my fingers into eternity without knowing about you.*

Keeping that promise had taken Terry on a journey he could never have imagined, with an assignment he might never have accepted. He had been through valleys so deep as to look into demons' eyes, and climbed mountains so high as to glimpse the back of God. And yet....

Here he was, not fleeing a mob, or praying with a Pope, or petitioning a President, but sitting at table with a humble Iraqi family whose little boy, just a few seats away, was basking in his father's love. Here—all around this table—was real grace. Not the threatening truce Terry had lived under as a boy who could never keep its terms, nor the cheap, get-out-of-jail-free card that had replaced it in pop culture. Here was grace alive, the savory feast for all mankind that too few enjoyed.

Here was Jesus.

We're in the eye! That's where we are. We're in the eye of the storm, because that's where God's presence is. The storms always surround us, but we live in the eye. Here is where we live in His presence... the only thing that can hold us through every storm.

Terry looked out the second story window at the street below, its surface shining from a mist too fine to see.

No storms here tonight, he thought. But he knew that somewhere they raged on.[1]

Cake and coffee were served, and then the party drew to an end. It was late and time to sleep. The food had been good—Greek food always was—but tonight it had become a Communion, perhaps as holy a convocation as any Terry had ever known.

The party of nine stepped out into the mist, Terry and Jamal leading the way, with Nabil and Pastor Sameh following at the rear. In between, Amina and the children maintained some distance from Jamal, not that they feared him in any way, but according to ageless custom. Kurdish women simply did not walk with men.

But the group had not gone half a block when Terry felt an arm slip under his own, as an umbrella was raised over his head. Amina had broken the rules, not merely by walking forward, but by touching a man who was not her husband.

Terry looked at her. She said nothing, but only smiled.

She doesn't want me to get wet, realized Terry. *She's flouting timeless custom, just to protect me from a little drizzle.*

Tonight, for once in his life, the Storm Chaser would stay dry. And as he thought about it, Terry realized that there was no more engaging, exciting place on earth he would rather be than right here, right now.

Almost...

---

[1] In fact, if Terry could have seen past the buildings and the land and the sea, he might have learned that on this very day, his Jubilee birthday, a new storm was beginning to brew, as a small but determined league of terrorists gathered somewhere in Syria, or perhaps in southern Turkey, to formally adopt their new name: ISIS. Terry would later confront this storm, in 2014.

EPILOGUE:
SAFE AT HOME

(J A M E S   G I L B E R T)

LEAVE IT TO ROMANCE to ruin a good ending.

I had fully intended to tell you about Jamal's complete healing a few weeks after our story left off, and of how he and Amina are happily ministering to the Kurdish community in another nation. But our adventure has been ambushed by "happily ever after."

Eight years ago, when I first suggested to Terry Law that someone should write his life story, he scoffed at the idea, saying that it would seem like bragging and, in any case, would serve no good purpose. I wasn't surprised. Terry was a single man whose sole mission in life was to reveal God's grace and mercy to oppressed and suffering people everywhere, no matter the cost. Such intense focus served him like a smelter that burns off dross to render gold. St. Paul's revelation that, "where sin increased, grace abounded all the more," came through the fire in Terry's mind reduced and refined: "Oppression equals opportunity."

Danger, if Terry noticed it at all, was a mosquito to flick from his arm. He was single and dedicated to staying that way, and his now adult children, all fully capable of living on their own, had accepted their father's calling, and the implicit possibility that any mission might be his last.

Having thus set his resolve, Terry was a hollow man, a vessel of hope for the world, holding none for himself. In ministry, he had told himself he was partnering with St. Paul: no wife—no obligations. But in reality, he was using Scripture to mask his fears: no love—no risk.

In 2007, we had temporarily suspended work on a joint re-write of Terry's 1987 internationally bestselling book, *The Power of Praise and Worship*, in order to take up his latest obsession: hope. We talked by phone nearly every day, and at all hours. He was most accessible after sunset, and if I caught him in the middle of an appointment, he would politely tell me so and return my call later.

Not so one particular summer evening.

"Terry, have you got a couple of minutes to go over something?"

"Uh, no Jim. I'm actually having dinner with someone."

"No problem. Just call me later, or tomorrow morning."

"Wait, Jim. There's someone I want you to meet. How would you like to say hello to the prettiest girl in Tulsa?"

In all the 38 years I had known Terry Law, never had I heard him speak in such a flirty voice. Seconds earlier he had been the Alberta cowboy turned Oral Roberts University regent, telling me he was in an appointment. Now he was goo.

"Hang on while I hand her the phone, Jim. This is Barbara Wolfer. She teaches English at ORU."

A rich alto voice quietly greeted me with a questioning "Hello" on the other end of the line. Even in that single word, a bit of Northeast dignity filtered through to my southern ears. Barbara and I exchanged the requisite pleasantries of two people with a mutual friend, and then she handed the phone back to Terry.

"Tell me everything," I commanded my mentor when he called the next day. "I've *never* heard you talk that way."

"Well, we met three years ago...."

What?

"She lives just two doors down."

What?

Writing took a one-hour holiday, as I plied my friend about his sudden change of personality. Oprah could not have done a better job, and he soon spilled the beans.

It was the end of February 2004, and although he had lived in his Tulsa neighborhood for a couple of years, Terry knew none of his immediate neighbors. Anyone wanting to meet him probably stood a better chance at the Tulsa airport.

"My daughter Becca came in one day and told me that our neighbor two doors down had just lost her husband," said Terry. "She suggested that since I had also suffered the loss of a spouse, I might offer to pray for the lady. So I did. And I gave her my phone number and told her I would be available for any counsel she might seek. We met once or twice over the next six weeks, and then we didn't really talk again for two years."

Terry often jogged in the afternoons, and occasionally he would greet Barbara if she happened to be outside gardening or checking her mail. But as two years became three, they both couldn't help noticing how often his jogging began to coincide with her mailbox checking.

"It was almost three years to the day since we had met, and I was outside playing football with my grandson, Taylor, when I saw Barbara at her mailbox," said Terry. "So I went over to say hi.

I thought I'd take a chance and ask her if she was seeing anyone. She said no, and asked the same of me. I told her no and started talking about how busy my schedule had been.

"She laughed and said, 'Well, with a schedule like that, no wonder you've haven't met anyone!' I liked her feisty attitude, and right then I asked her to have dinner with me."

Terry and Barbara were engaged shortly before Thanksgiving 2007, and were married on May 31, 2008. The whole weekend still lives in me, beginning with the rehearsal dinner the preceding evening in the garden of their future home.

Terry and Barbara had sold their two homes in favor of a spacious, brick two-story a couple of miles away. With nearly a hundred guests to serve, it was my first chance to see the bride-to-be in action. Barbara's grace, charm and engaging wit were, like her beloved garden, in full bloom. A hundred guests from half-a-dozen countries? No problem. A fiancé whose courage and strength of character were matched by his intellect? She was his equal.

Terry's and Barbara's wedding the next day, at a wooded hillside chapel north of town, began fifteen minutes late and a few guests short, thanks to a last-minute tornado that sliced across the city but did little damage. I had watched the ominous wall cloud forming over west Tulsa, as I paralleled it in my rental car on Highway 169. Despite our naming of storms, my nine years in Florida had never produced such a fearsome sight, and had the occasion been less historic I might have chosen shelter over a slice of wedding cake.

But this was Will Rogers' Oklahoma, and by the time the nuptials began, heaven's best blue sky and a canopy of green had given the chapel's arched windows their reason to be.

The two hundred of us who sat as witnesses to the solemn deed comprised a living sea of memories. Dennis Bjorgan, Terry's childhood friend who had been foolhardy enough to join him aboard a freighter to Africa in 1964, and Cheri, the girl who'd drawn him home. Joel Vesanen, always present and always faithful, across the aisle beside his equally faithful wife Ruth. Don Moen, who had set Terry's life message to music, and his wife Laura. Pastors Voth and Yandian, who had shepherded the bride and groom through life's darkest valleys. Ray Bevan, the Welshman who had pointed Terry to his future on a beach one day in Cyprus.

I confess that I do not remember much about the vows and rituals of that hour, nor the raft of tributes and speeches that followed in the hall next door. I cannot even recall which classical piece Larry Dalton played at the Steinway, other than to say that J.S. Bach must have rejoiced on high that somebody had finally gotten him right.

What I do remember is simply this: Two hundred souls sat in wonder, many cried, and everyone laughed out loud, as grace played out before our eyes.

I have spent the better part of these pages telling you the story of Terry Law, the Storm Chaser. Even now, it is an adventure half told, and better than a tall tale, as I told him the other day. But the best part of Terry's story is Barbara.

She is not Mrs. Storm Chaser. She is Barbara Law. She can travel, but prefers tulips. She is not afraid of a platform, but would sooner be in a classroom. She favors students over celebrities, Dickens over Dr. Phil, books over movies, and loves—absolutely loves—the New York Yankees, Oklahoma Thunder, OU Sooner football, and Duster, her timid gray cat. Most of all, she loves her husband, a man named Terry, and their seven children.

For twenty years, Barbara was the mother of one: a fine young man named David. But in becoming Mrs. Terry Law on that last day in May, she also gave herself to his six—Misty, Scot, Shawna, Jason, Rebecca, and Laurie—instantly becoming a mother and grandmother in the process. I say "instantly" for good reason: from the very first, Barbara has done more than love Terry's children *like* a mother. She has *been* their mother, bringing love and healing to each as though she had always been there, from the first scraped knee to the latest award. It is a ministry to which she is as well suited as Terry is to chasing storms.

Equally gratifying is Terry's passionate commitment to his seventh child and third son, David Wolfer. As a seasoned man of God, Terry is determined to pass along to all his sons the fortitude and pioneer spirit of his own father, Bert Law, while taking care to add the affirmation that for so long he lacked. In response, David's respect for his mom's new husband has grown into a son's affection.

364 days after Terry and Barbara were married, a sleeping Larry Dalton abruptly left earth for heaven. One week later a symphony orchestra, a 300-voice choir and a hastily reconstituted Living Sound were joined by nearly two thousand people who gathered in Tulsa to honor Larry's life. That evening, 150 LS alumni and longtime friends of Terry's descended on the Law residence for an impromptu reunion.

I watched Barbara that evening, as we all moved from group to group inside the house and out by the pool, regaling one another with tales about Larry, life on the road, and honest-to-goodness miracles overseas. These were stories she did not know, and memories she could not share. It could not have been easy for her, but no one knew. Because she was Barbara.

You know by now, I'm sure, that Terry's story continues. As I write, he has recently returned from Irbil, Kurdistan, in what used to be Iraq. The terror force called ISIS was encamped some 20 miles away, awaiting their chance to attack, when Terry and his son Jason, who is succeeding him as World Compassion's president, arrived on scene and began distributing the first of 700,000 meals subsequently delivered to the refugees that had overwhelmed the capital.

That story and more will be told at some point, I'm sure. But I am mentioning it only briefly now, if you'll bear with me, in order to tell you one more thing.

There was a time when one might say that "Terry recently returned from" some far corner of the earth, only to begin the next sentence with, "and will soon be going to" another corner. But no longer. Now Terry returns *home*. Home to Barbara and gardening and grandkids and all of the life he used to fear. No more going off somewhere in order to *not* be here. He comes home.

It would be easy for you to think that Barbara's part in this thrill-a-minute true adventure is the kiss before the credits roll, but it is not. Far from being the angel atop this Christmas tree, she is its base, that hidden anchor behind all the presents, holding the whole thing up while the family gathers around.

That is what makes Terry's story worth telling, and I hope it is what you'll take away. Some Storm Chasers live only for the chase, but the best come home to live.

JAMES GILBERT is an author and speaker who has ministered in sixty-one nations on five continents, with special emphasis on Cuba and Eastern Europe.

James has presented the gospel of Jesus Christ in every kind of setting. He has lectured in Moscow's City Hall, sung the blues at a Soviet jazz festival, conducted medical clinics in China, taught Iraqi church leaders, slept on thousands of beds and floors and been served, as he puts it, "every type of food from fine French cuisine to cow skin."

James has written four books, beginning with *How a Man Stands Up for Christ*, published by Bethany House Publishers in 1996. He also co-authored two books with Dr. Terry Law: *The Power of Praise and Worship,* and *The Hope Habit* (Charisma House, 2010).

He has also written dozens of songs and recorded three full albums, including Integrity's Hosanna! Music worship CD, *Lamb of God.*

James lives with his wife and daughter in Florida.

ACKNOWLEDGMENTS

Although this book represents three years of research and dozens of face-to-face interviews conducted from the southeastern U.S.A. to southwestern Canada, two people to whom I am particularly indebted have already received a greater reward. If indeed heaven's great cloud of witnesses is somehow allowed to monitor our earthly progress, then both Ann Law, Terry's mother, and Oral Roberts deserve a fist-pump of thanks for their insights into my subject's childhood and early ministry.

Deepest thanks, as well, to Terry's family, both immediate and extended, for trusting me to intrude a bit further into your lives than I had a right to expect. His pride in you is well deserved.

The middle chapters of this book comprise the "Living Sound" years, and if space permitted, I would thank each of the group's 350 alumni by name. Both Terry Law and I are richer men for having served God with you.

David Hazard, director of ASCENT, is more than the writing and publishing coach who taught me a new genre—he's a true and patient friend and a treasure to anyone fortunate enough to be taken under his mentoring wing.

Finally, thank you to my true love, Dolly, who has not only stood by me during our 39 years of marriage, but has carried me a good bit of the time, as well, and to our daughter, Lexi, who has sacrificed several Saturday morning dates and a couple of summer vacations, so Daddy could do a good job. The two of you are the sweetest and most perfect of God's gifts.

CHASER
PRINCIPLES TO GUIDE YOU

Chapter 1: Clouded Heart
When your life is not in God's hands, the greatest storm is the one inside you. You were created to let his life and will flow through you, not to resist him.

Chapter 2: Rebel with a Call
When you resist God, your call "feels" like a terrible storm, and you want to run from it. But running from God exposes you to real turmoil and potential devastation.

Chapter 3: First Light
You want to serve God, but you feel un-qualified: "I'm nobody. What if I fail?" But say "Yes" and God will bring that calling to pass. Grace is there when you need it.

Chapter 4: The Desert
When you seek direction, God will keep you waiting until you come to know his voice. That sound is more important than information. Relationship means everything.

Chapter 5: Training Day
Seek and keep on seeking and you shall find; knock and keep on knocking and it shall be opened...just not where you expected.

Chapter 6: Out of Africa
When your dreams of serving God appear to have been dashed and all hope seems lost, that is when God will step in to show you that only he can bring to pass what he has called you to do.

Chapter 7: Crack in the Curtain
When you have trusted God and conquered one storm, another will be waiting. Because grace only grows when the storms grow too.

Chapter 8: Storm on Purpose
When you've grown in God's grace, you'll also walk into storms you used to avoid, because you have confidence God will meet you there. This is a measure of maturity.

Chapter 9: The Evil Empire
Even when your good intentions have gotten you in over your head, God will give you wisdom to navigate the toughest of storms.

Chapter 10: If I Make My Bed in Hell
When you have served God faithfully, unexpected storms may threaten to bring you down. But God will give you strength for every storm, especially when your own strength is gone.

Chapter 11: Aftermath
Even if you have been marked by shame, your reputation has been shattered and your friends are gone, God remains faithful. Having lost everything and still trusted God, you are truly free.

Chapter 12: Storm of the Century
When the whole world has gone dark around you, light your one lone candle. It will shine more brightly than you ever imagined.

Chapter 13: Escape
When you dare to face danger in Jesus' name, God will honor that name. Even when the storm threatens your very life, God is with you, and will bring you out as surely as he took you in.

Chapter 14: The Accidental Ambassador
When you place your life fully in God's hands, you will stand restfully in his presence, no matter how hard the storms of life rage around you. You will live in the eye.

Chapter 15: Out of the Storms
When you allow God to hollow "self" out, you become your true self, his vessel of grace for your world. You can face any storm with strength and peace.